THE MESSAGE OF THE TAPE

An Easy to Understand, Easy to Remember Illumination of the Movements of Stock Prices

By
Martin J. Favino

Copyright 2011 by Martin J. Favino

ISBN-13: 978-1534882058

ISBN-10: 1534882057

Edited By
Robert Pirillo

Dedication

This book is dedicated to anyone and everyone who ever wanted to understand the message contained within the movements of stock prices. *Yes, the fluctuations of stock prices are in fact sending a message.* That message is *The Message Of The Tape.* The message is, if you know what to look for, revealing *when to buy and when to sell.*

It is also dedicated to the life lived of someone I'll never meet, Jesse Lauriston Livermore, the greatest stock operator who ever lived.

TABLE OF CONTENTS

FOREWORD

This book is named **The Message Of The Tape** in honor of the turn of the century era of the great stock operators when stock prices were printed on the ***ticker tape*** of yesteryear. When read by a skilled and experienced tape reader, "the tape" revealed clear, unmistakable price patterns on which those bold and daring stock operators based their trades. Those unmistakable price patterns, that is, Rallies, Reactions, Trends and Pivotal Points compose *The Message Of The Tape*.

Rallies, Reactions, Trends and Pivotal Points have all been around for a long time but what has been missing is a realistic, simple, ***consistent, universal, standardi-zation of measurement*** that quickly, easily and accurately identifies these movements. ***That method of measurement must be applicable today and any time in the future to all stocks at any price.*** It has to have the flexibility and accuracy to allow us to identify where a stock is today within one of these movements and where it may be going.

This book provides that consistent, universal and standardized measurement plus a lot more.

But that's only half the story. Once such a system of measurement is applied, just like the great stock operators, we need to be able to interpret and understand what each movement means and the part each plays in the overall ***message of the tape***. Understanding ***the message of tape*** means understanding ***the message*** that these movements compose so that you can form an opinion as to when you may be given a signal to buy or to sell.

This method of measurement allows each individual stock itself to tell us when it is in or approaching a Rally, Reaction or Trend. It is applicable to all commodities, currencies, indices, index funds, mutual funds, exchange traded funds (ETFs) and preferred stocks. *The Message Of The Tape is exactly the same for all of them.*

Is this you?

1. You worked hard and honest your whole life, you trusted your broker and his firm. They were in a large, beautiful building and they have great T.V. commercials. You bought what and when they told you to buy. You lost. You lost big. They never told you to sell. Worried and nervous, you asked questions. They told you to "hang in there" or "ride it out" or "it will come back." But it didn't.

2. Your brokers bought and sold for you on your behalf. You lost.

3. You were in a 401k at work. You had a fair amount of hard earned money that you were counting on for your retirement. Maybe that 401k was actually made up of the stock of the company you worked for. You watched it carefully, believed the rumors of how well it was doing, the price seemed to go up. Then it began to go down. You were unsure of the decline so you sold that stock and kept it in the cash portion of the plan. Suddenly, the stock rose and you felt it was too late to get back in or too expensive or, you were just plain apprehensive.

4. You have been "had" so many times in the market that you decided to go it on your own. That is, buying and selling. You met with disaster.

5. You tried investing in everything from cotton to natural gas. You read and studied everything, but somehow you lost.

6. You bought expensive software that was supposed to indicate when to buy and sell. You lost.

If you fall into any of the categories above, you can benefit from this book.

Is this also you?

1. You would like to know what the signals are that indicate your stock may be going up or down.

2. You would like to know what signals indicate that your stock is only in a rally or reaction and may change direction or keep going in its present direction.

3. You want to read a short, simple book, like this, and then be able to forevermore read a stock chart *at a glance* and have a good idea what's happening.

4. ***You want an easy to learn method that requires no complicated calculations at all and can be remembered easily without having to refer to a computer program or anything else except a simple stock chart.***

Who else can benefit from this book?

Even if you know absolutely nothing about the overall market(s), stocks, indexes and commodities, or if you are an experienced investor, by taking a little time to learn this simple method you will be able to guide yourself regarding stock prices and overall market movements.

This book is not an investment advice tool, it won't tell you what to buy. You need to decide that for yourself. But once you are acquainted with ***The Message Of The Tape*** you will be able to see clearly when you ***may*** be given a signal when to buy, when to sell, when to hold or when to stay on the sidelines with cash until the signal arrives.

INTRODUCTION

There is No More Ticker Tape

The practice or art of **reading the tape** was the very first skill mastered by many if not all of the great stock operators. **The Message Of The Tape** is how they built their great stock fortunes. A closely guarded secret, each one of them had their own unique system of measurement and of interpretation as well. But in those days, there were fewer stocks. Perhaps 100 or so and the tape moved relatively slowly so the message was easier to spot. **The Message still exists today and it is exactly the same message as in the early days.** Although it is all but impossible to see amid the blur of 10,000 stocks plus commodities, indices, exchange traded funds (ETF) and currencies, all of which stream by too quickly. In some stocks, 200 million shares or more are traded each day. By the sheer power of technology and volume the speed of today's "Tape" is now so fast that the message is invisible. However, with the use of good charts and the methods shown in this book, the message can "be seen by the naked eye." Easily understood, **The Message Of The Tape** is there for anyone to see.

As stated in the Dedication, the fluctuations of stock prices are, in fact, sending a message. ***The Message Of The Tape*** is a unique and simple method of measuring and interpreting the repetitive movements of stock prices to reveal that message. ***The Message Of The Tape allows us to form an opinion as to where that stock is today and where it may be going in the future.*** Understanding these movements and patterns is like understanding a different language or a musical score. The "tape" has been repeating these same movements and composing the same message from the very first moment that stocks were traded until today and it will continue to do this as long as stocks are traded. Once you are able to see and understand ***The Message Of The Tape*** you will be able to look at a stock chart and in a few seconds understand where your stock is within one of these movements. You will also be alert to and have a good understanding of ***what it is telling you today about where it may be heading in the future***.

These patterns are surprisingly easy to reveal, simple in fact; anyone can do it and this book shows you how. ***No math is required***.

The Message Of The Tape will show you quickly and simply how to recognize the following important patterns:

1. Upward trends

2. Downward trends

3. Rallies

4. Reactions

5. When an upward trend has ended and may be transforming into a downward trend.

6. When a downward trend has ended and may be transforming into an upward trend.

7. When an upward or downward trend is experiencing only a rally or reaction and that the present trend may resume.

More importantly, *The Message Of The Tape* will explain how to interpret the above movements *of any individual stock itself* to reveal when your *stock itself* may be signaling when to buy or when to sell.

The easiest way to observe these movements is through the use of charts. *Charts reveal The Message Of The Tape in the simplest and easiest way possible*. There is also a spreadsheet version which is included later in this book.

The Message Of The Tape is actually two messages simultaneously. The first message is the overall *trend* and the second message is the smaller movements within that trend known as *rallies* and *reactions*. See fig 5 below. The important question as we look at figure 5 is: what are the signals and the system of measurement that would help us identify when that downward trend was reversing to an upward trend and visa versa?

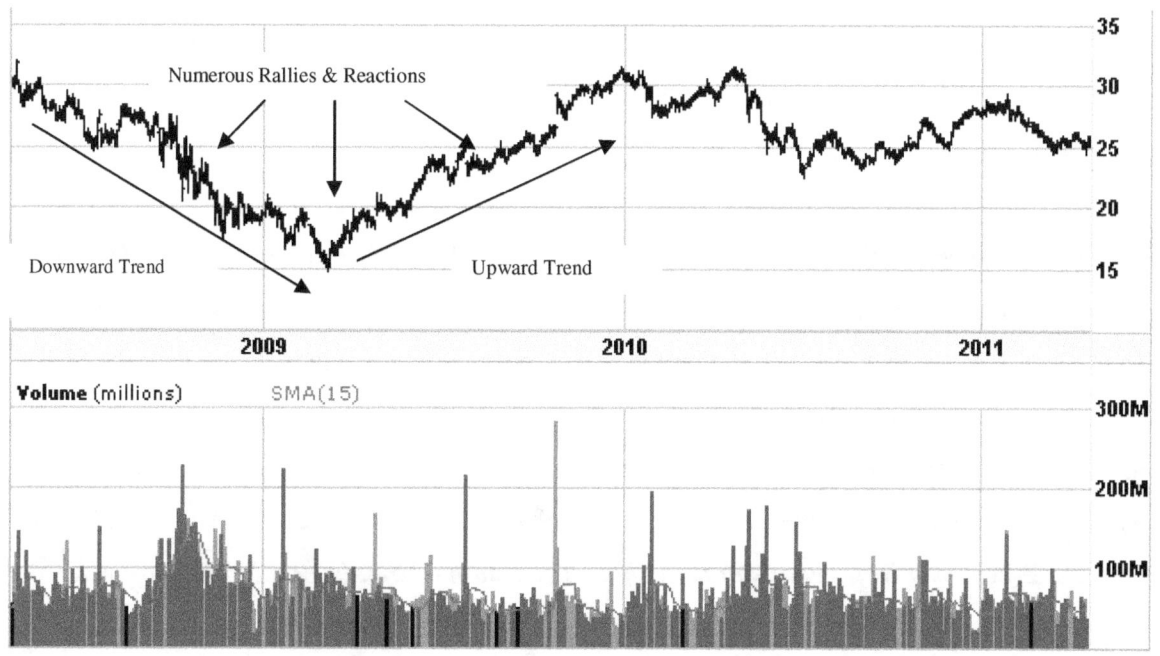

Diagram 5   Microsoft 3 yr. Thank You Etrade

In this short book we will explore all of these in detail.

One thing to remember as you read this book is that when we say "stock" we also mean *all* commodities, currencies, indices, index funds, mutual funds, exchange traded funds (ETF) and preferred stocks. *The Message Of The Tape is exactly the same for all of them*.

CHAPTER 1

Measurement

The Daily price movement is the new measurement

In order to reveal and interpret The Message Of The Tape there needs to be a consistent, universal, standardized unit of measurement that we can rely on in order to identify the beginnings and ends of rallies, reactions and trends.

That unit of measurement is the *daily** high and low price of a stock. *The action of the daily high and low price creates rallies and reactions.* Rallies and reactions are created *at specific times* when the high of a day is lower than the low of a previous day, or the low of a day is higher than the high of a previous day (see Figures A and B below). This signals *at specific times* that a rally, reaction or trend has begun and a previous rally, reaction or trend has ended. Rallies and reactions in turn create *pivotal points.* Pivotal points are the *extreme prices high or low* of rallies, reactions and trends (see Figures A and B below). *Pivotal points in turn signal the action of trends…and trends are where the money is.* Understanding *rallies, reactions* and *pivotal points* is the first step to understanding *The Message Of The Tape*.

How the Daily Price movement creates Rallies, Reactions & Pivotal Points

Figures A and B below show how the daily high and low price creates rallies and reactions which in turn create pivotal points.

* Weekly, Monthly and Yearly can also be used.

Figure A :
Daily high and low creates Rally and Low Pivotal Point

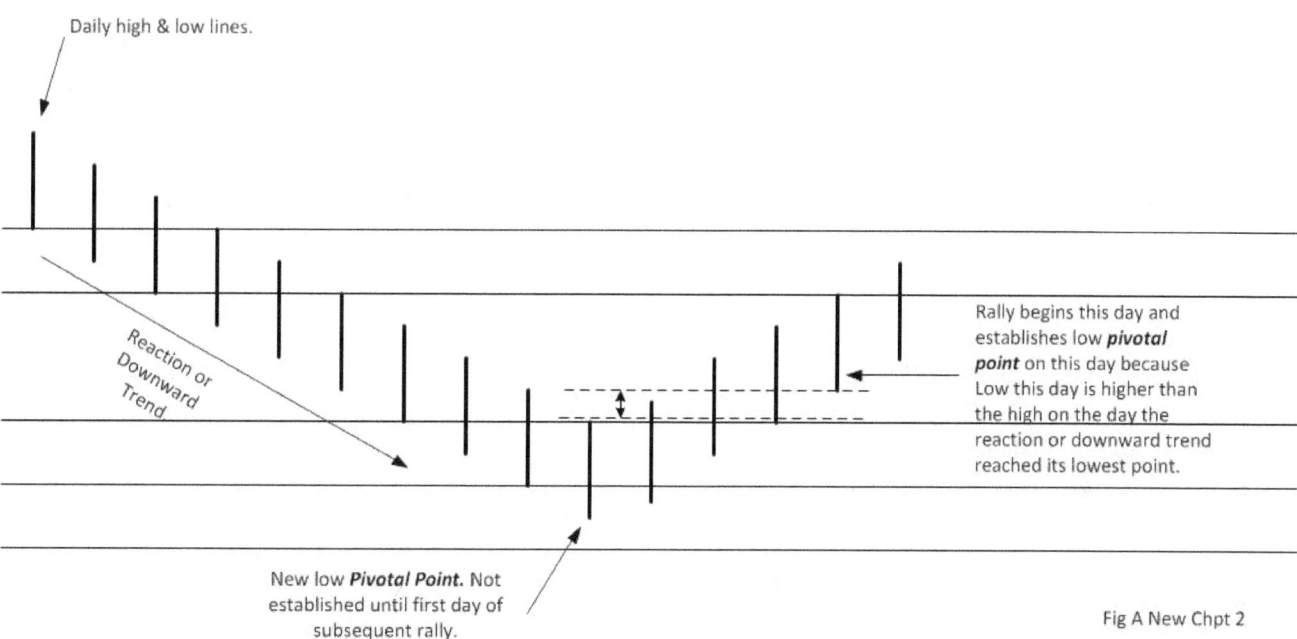

Daily high & low lines.

Reaction or Downward Trend.

Rally begins this day and establishes low **pivotal point** on this day because Low this day is higher than the high on the day the reaction or downward trend reached its lowest point.

New low **Pivotal Point.** Not established until first day of subsequent rally.

Fig A New Chpt 2

In Figure A above, we see how the movement of the daily high and low price creates a rally after a downward movement. _**The first day of the rally simultaneously establishes the low pivotal point.**_ Because we never know how low a stock will go or how long it will continue to go down, we can not recognize the low pivotal point until the price has moved enough in the _**opposite direction**_ to create, in this case, a rally. This means that in Figure A we cannot recognize the low pivotal point until _**the first day of the rally**_ which occurs several days later. Observing the action of the daily high and low price, we see in Figure A above, the rally begins on the first day the low of the day is higher than the high of the day that the reaction reached its lowest point.

Pivotal points are not formed until the first day of a subsequent rally or reaction even though they actually occur before a rally or reaction.

<u>Looking at Figure A above, in the case of a downward movement a rally occurs:</u>

- After a stock has reached its lowest point of a reaction or downward trend.
- After the price begins to move upward.
- A rally is in the making on the first day the low price is higher than the high price on the day the reaction or downward trend reaches its lowest point. That lowest point is known as the ***pivotal point***.
- The low pivotal point is not established as the low point of that particular movement until the rally begins.

The same rules apply to upward trends and rallies except the movement is opposite as in Figure B below.

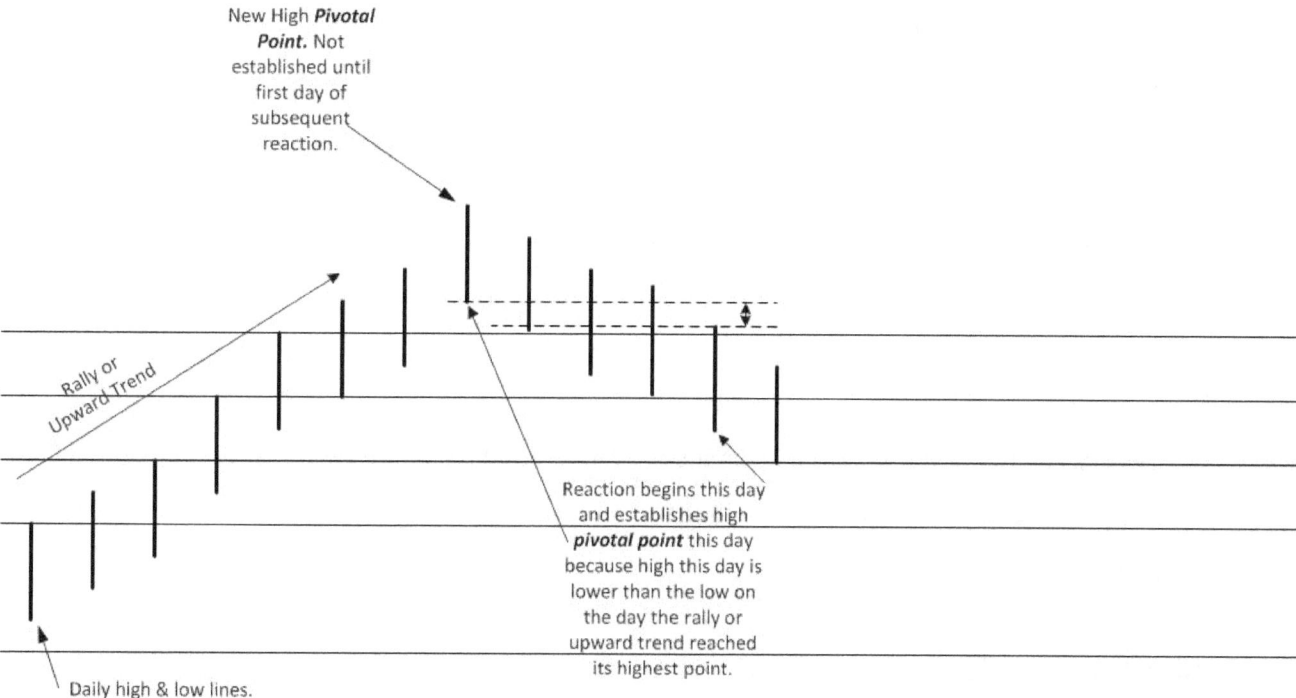

New High *Pivotal Point.* Not established until first day of subsequent reaction.

Rally or Upward Trend

Reaction begins this day and establishes high *pivotal point* this day because high this day is lower than the low on the day the rally or upward trend reached its highest point.

Daily high & low lines.

Fig B New Chpt 2

In Figure B above, we see how the movement of the daily high and low price creates a reaction after an upward movement. ***The first day of the reaction simultaneously establishes the high pivotal point.*** Because we never know how high a stock will go or how long it will continue to go up, we do not recognize a high pivotal point until the price has moved enough in the ***opposite direction*** to create, in this case, a reaction. This means that in Figure B we cannot recognize the high pivotal point until ***the first day of the reaction*** which occurs several days later. Observing the action of the daily high and low price, we see in Figure B above, the reaction begins on the first day the high of the day is lower than the low on the day that the rally reached its highest point.

<u>Looking at Figure B above, in the case of an upward movement, a reaction occurs when:</u>

- After a stock reaches its highest point of a rally or upward trend.
- After the price begins to move downward.
- A reaction is in the making on the first day the high price is lower than the low price on the day the rally or upward trend reached its highest point. That highest point is known as the *pivotal point*.
- The high pivotal point is not established as the high point of that particular movement until the reaction begins.

Because a rally or reaction can occur at any point throughout a movement, a resulting pivotal point can occur anywhere as well. *Again, it is the subsequent rally or reaction that creates the pivotal point.*

Next, looking at Figure C, we see the formation of several high and low pivotal points as a result of several rallies and reactions.

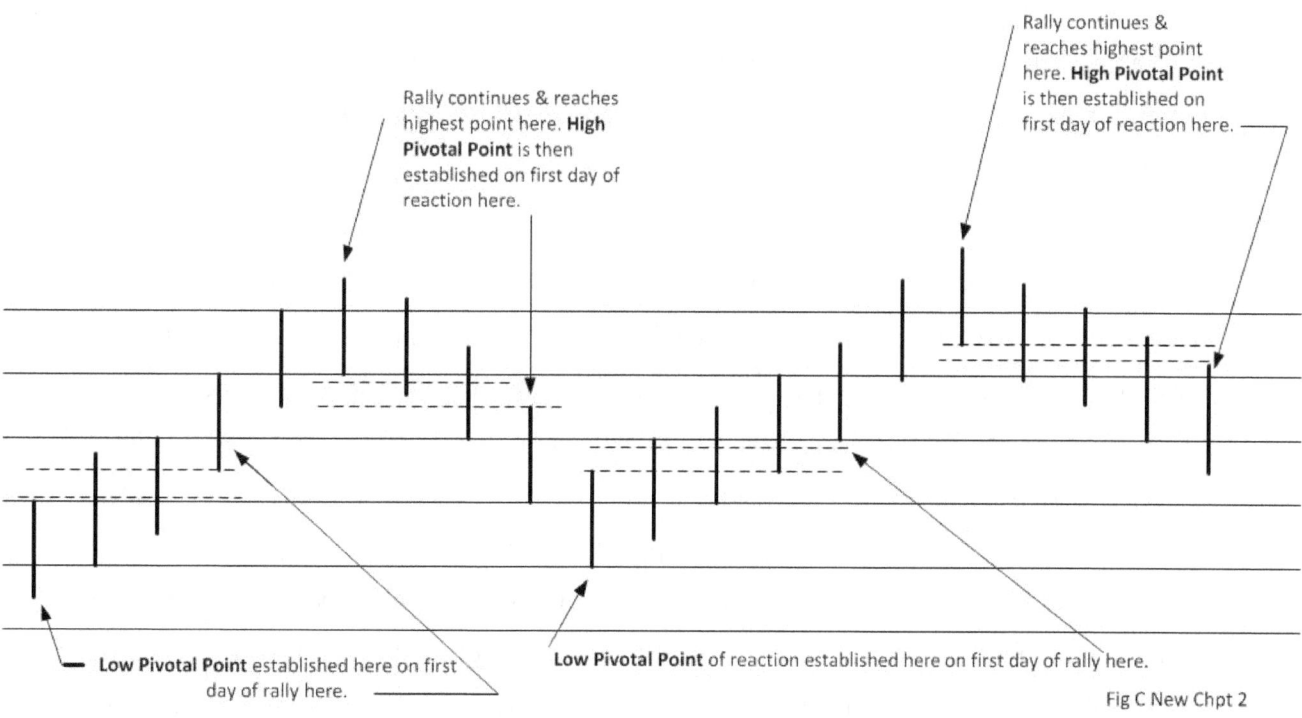

Figure C showing how rallies and reactions create multiple pivotal points as a result of the daily price movement.

Rally continues & reaches highest point here. **High Pivotal Point** is then established on first day of reaction here.

Rally continues & reaches highest point here. **High Pivotal Point** is then established on first day of reaction here.

Low Pivotal Point established here on first day of rally here.

Low Pivotal Point of reaction established here on first day of rally here.

Fig C New Chpt 2

We can see as stated earlier, that the movements of prices are composing a message, *The Message Of The Tape*. *The Message Of The Tape* is made up of rallies, reactions, pivotal points and trends which are all *created and measured by the daily action of the high and low price*. Next, we will begin to put these movements together to completely understand what *The Message Of The Tape* is saying.

CHAPTER 2

Understanding Pivotal Points

In Chapter 1, we explored the fundamental measurement of rallies reactions and how they form pivotal points. ***Pivotal points are the key sign posts and are the single most important element of The Message Of The Tape.***

As we have seen in Chapter 1, a pivotal point is formed on the first day of a subsequent rally or reaction. A pivotal point is called a pivotal point because it is an important price point in the movement of a stock. A pivotal point actually marks a specific price. It does this because it is formed when prices move enough in the opposite direction to create it.(See Fig A, B, C, Chapter 1) What a pivotal point is saying is the stock, for now, has gone as far as its going to go in that direction. And that's important. Why is it important? Because if the pivotal point is the high of a rally or upward trend, it means that buyers were not willing to pay more for it at that price and it began to sell off enough that it created a reaction. If it was the low of a reaction or downward trend, it means that buyers were willing to pay more for it and it stopped selling off at that price and the price began to rise enough to create a rally. But ***why*** is that important? It's important because when the stock returns to near that pivotal point, that is when you are going to find out how the buyers and sellers feel about the price of that stock. And that's ***very*** important. That is when you are going to find out if there is enough buying or selling momentum to pierce the pivotal point and keep going or if it will stop again and move in the opposite direction again.

In this chapter we will learn how to use pivotal points and the daily price movement to identify the following:

1. Trend Continuations
2. Beginnings and Ends of Trends
3. Trend Reversals

A *trend* begins, continues or reverses whenever the *pivotal point* of a rally, reaction or trend is pierced by the proper amount. The "proper amount" is the same daily high and low unit of measurement that is used to identify rallies, reactions and pivotal points (figures A, B, C - Chapter 1).

1.   How to Recognize Trend Continuations

- ### *How to Recognize an Upward Trend Continuation*

  The way to recognize an upward trend continuation is whenever a stock is already in an upward trend and establishes a high pivotal as a result of a subsequent reaction. The reaction is then followed by a rally but *the rally continues higher and breaks through the upward trend pivotal point by the proper amount.* See Figure F below. When it does this and the low of the day is higher than the high pivotal point of the upward trend, this indicates that the upward trend has resumed.

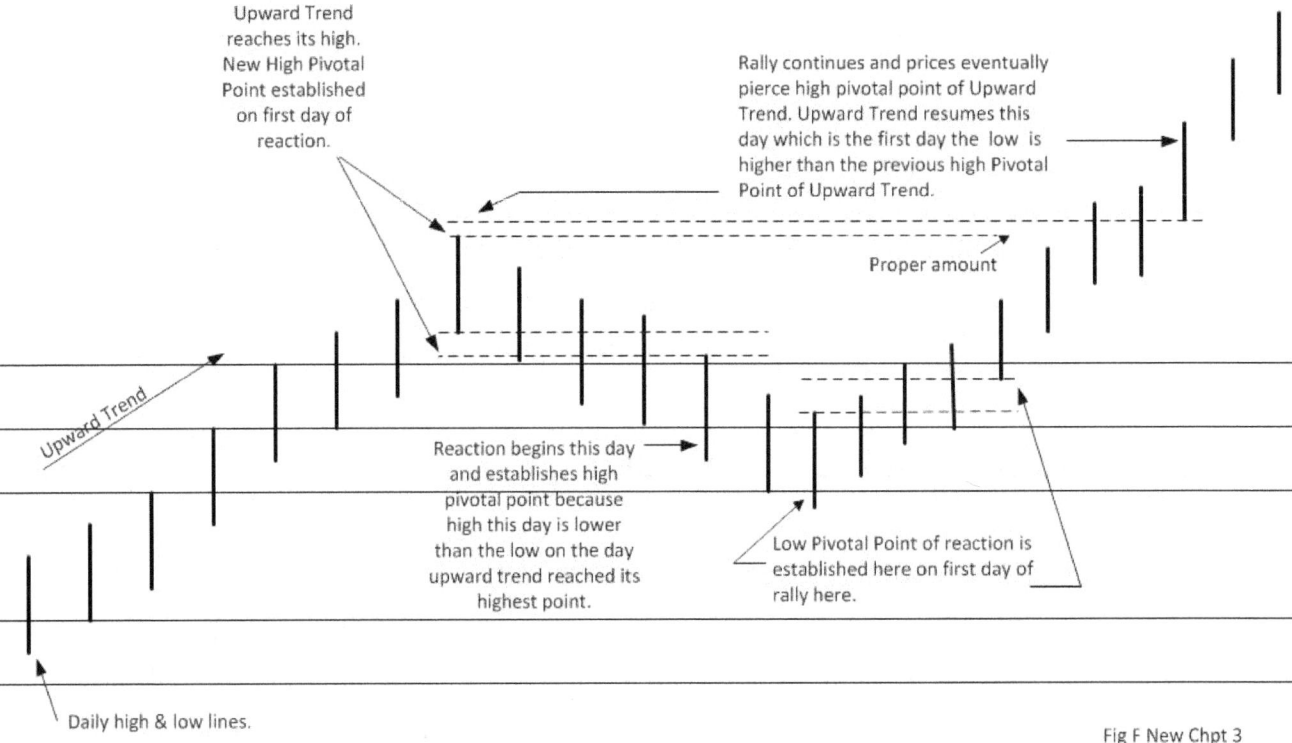

Figure F *showing upward trend continues because high pivotal point has been pierced by the proper amount.*

Upward Trend reaches its high. New High Pivotal Point established on first day of reaction.

Rally continues and prices eventually pierce high pivotal point of Upward Trend. Upward Trend resumes this day which is the first day the low is higher than the previous high Pivotal Point of Upward Trend.

Proper amount

Upward Trend

Reaction begins this day and establishes high pivotal point because high this day is lower than the low on the day upward trend reached its highest point.

Low Pivotal Point of reaction is established here on first day of rally here.

Daily high & low lines.

Fig F New Chpt 3

- ### _How to Recognize a Downward Trend Continuation_

The way to recognize a downward trend continuation is whenever a stock establishes a low pivotal point as a result of a subsequent rally. The rally is followed by a reaction but ***the reaction continues lower and breaks through the downward trend pivotal point by the proper amount.*** See Figure E below. When it does this and the high of the day is lower than the low pivotal point of the downward trend, this indicates that the downward trend has resumed.

Figure E showing downward trend continues because low pivotal
point has been pierced by the proper amount.

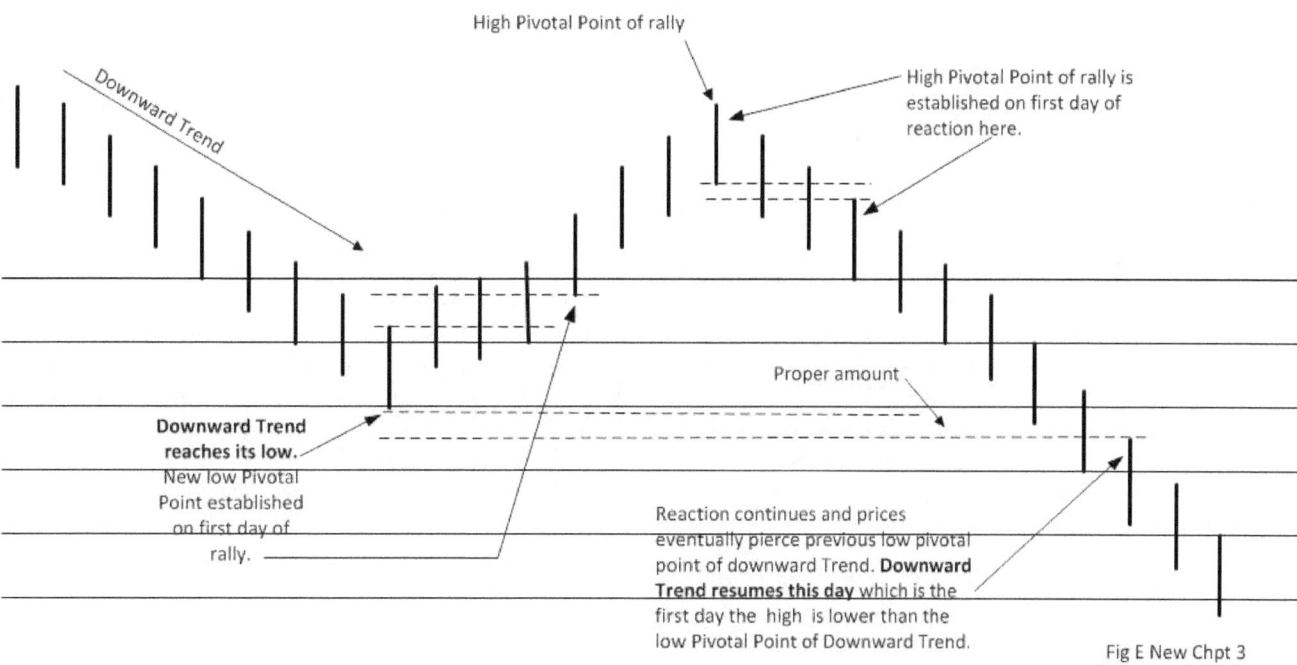

High Pivotal Point of rally

High Pivotal Point of rally is
established on first day of
reaction here.

Downward Trend

Proper amount

**Downward Trend
reaches its low.**

New low Pivotal
Point established
on first day of
rally.

Reaction continues and prices
eventually pierce previous low pivotal
point of downward Trend. **Downward
Trend resumes this day** which is the
first day the high is lower than the
low Pivotal Point of Downward Trend.

Fig E New Chpt 3

2.   How to Recognize Beginnings and Ends of Trends

*A **new trend begins*** whenever the most recent pivotal point of a ***rally or reaction*** is pierced by the proper amount.

- ### *How to Recognize When a New Upward Trend begins*

In Figure C.1 below we see how a new upward trend begins when the most recent pivotal point, in this case a rally, is pierced by the proper amount.

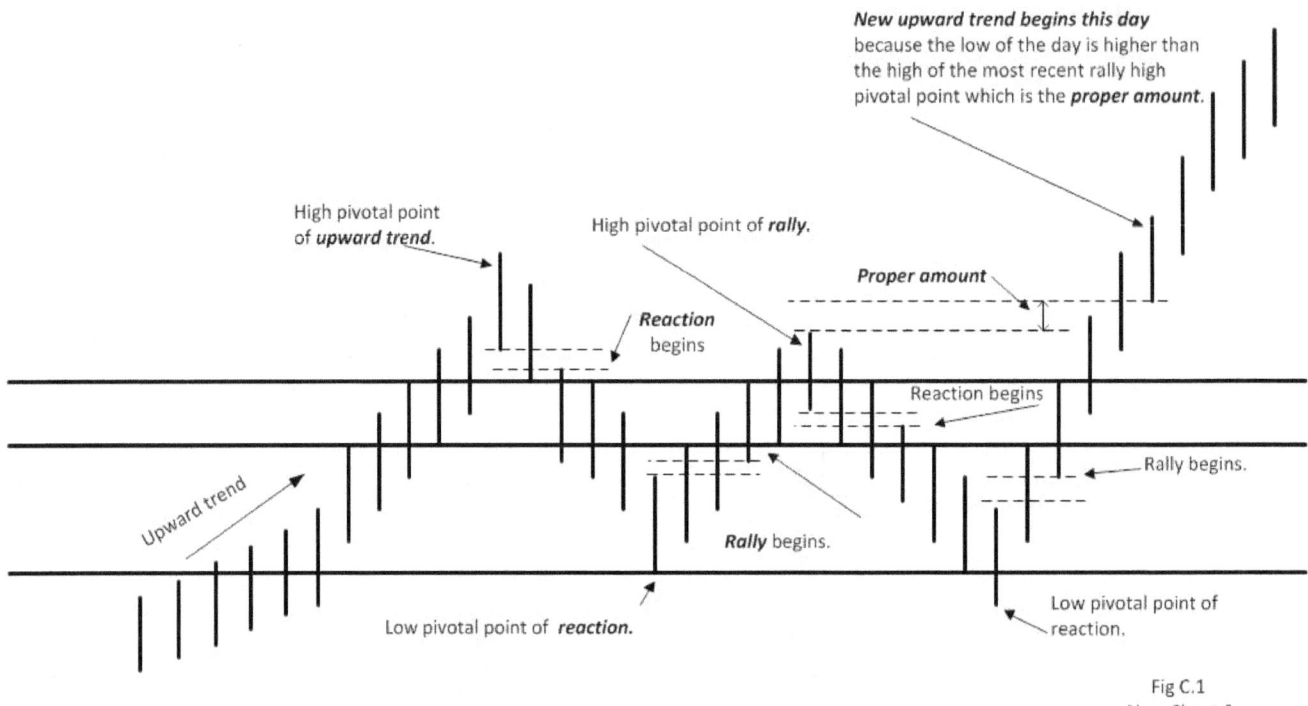

Figure C.1 *showing New upward trend beginning after rally pivotal point was pierced by proper amount.*

New upward trend begins this day because the low of the day is higher than the high of the most recent rally high pivotal point which is the *proper amount*.

High pivotal point of *upward trend*.

High pivotal point of *rally*.

Proper amount

Reaction begins

Reaction begins

Rally begins.

Upward trend

Rally begins.

Low pivotal point of *reaction*.

Low pivotal point of reaction.

Fig C.1
New Chapt 3

- ### *How to Recognize When a New Downward Trend Begins*

In Figure C.2 below we see how a new downward trend begins when the most recent pivotal point, in this case a reaction, is pierced by the proper amount.

22

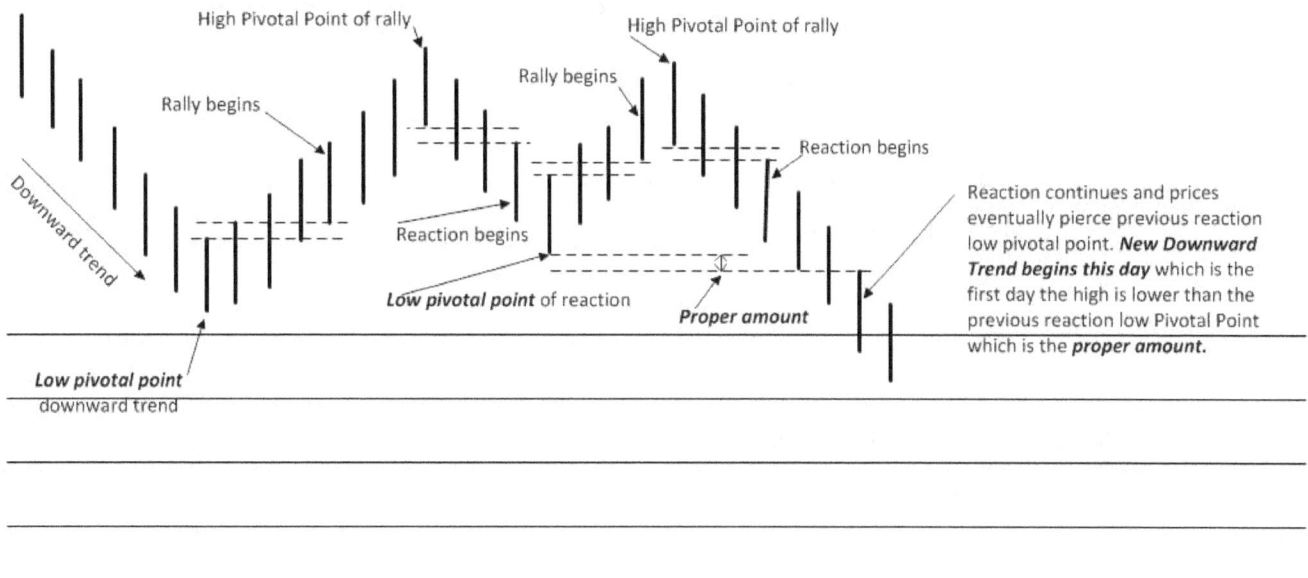

Figure C.2 showing New downward trend beginning after previous reaction pivotal point was pierced by proper amount.

Fig C.2 New Chpt 3

A trend is usually but not always a larger movement than a rally or reaction in both price and time, see Figure 5, Chapter one. Trends usually *contain rallies and reactions. We have already seen in the figures above that Trends begin and end when prices break through a previous rally or reaction pivotal point by the same daily high & low measurement that is used to create rallies & reactions. Even though a trend experiences a rally or reaction it remains in that trend until a pivotal point is crossed whereby it continues its present trend or reverses its trend.*

In Figures A, B, C, E, F above, we saw how pivotal points and the daily price unit of measurement are used to identify the beginnings and continuation of trends. Next, let's look at how the same system of measurement is used to determine *trend reversals.*

3. *How to Recognize Trend Reversals*

As stated in the beginning of this chapter: A trend is created, continued or ***reversed*** whenever the pivotal point of a rally, reaction or trend is pierced by the proper amount.

A reversal of trend is actually two events simultaneously. It is the beginning of a new trend and the end of the previous trend. However, the new trend is in the opposite direction of the previous trend.

Figure C.3 below shows a reversal of trend from an upward trend to a downward trend. The downward trend begins on the first day the high of the day is lower than the pivotal point of the most recent reaction.

Figure C.3 showing trend reversal after Upward Trend. Upward trend ends and downward trend begins

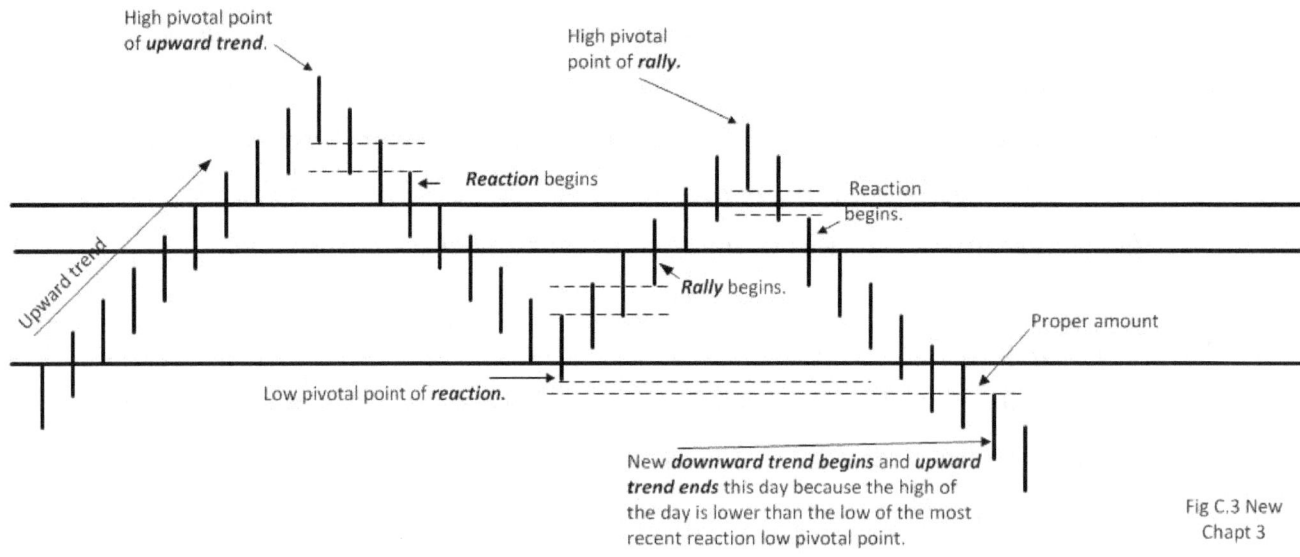

High pivotal point of **upward trend**.

High pivotal point of **rally.**

Reaction begins

Reaction begins.

Rally begins.

Proper amount

Upward trend

Low pivotal point of **reaction**.

New ***downward trend begins*** and **upward trend ends** this day because the high of the day is lower than the low of the most recent reaction low pivotal point.

Fig C.3 New Chapt 3

Figure C.4 below shows a reversal of trend from a downward trend to an upward trend. The downward trend ends on the same day the upward trend begins which is on the first day the low of the day is higher than the pivotal point of the most recent rally

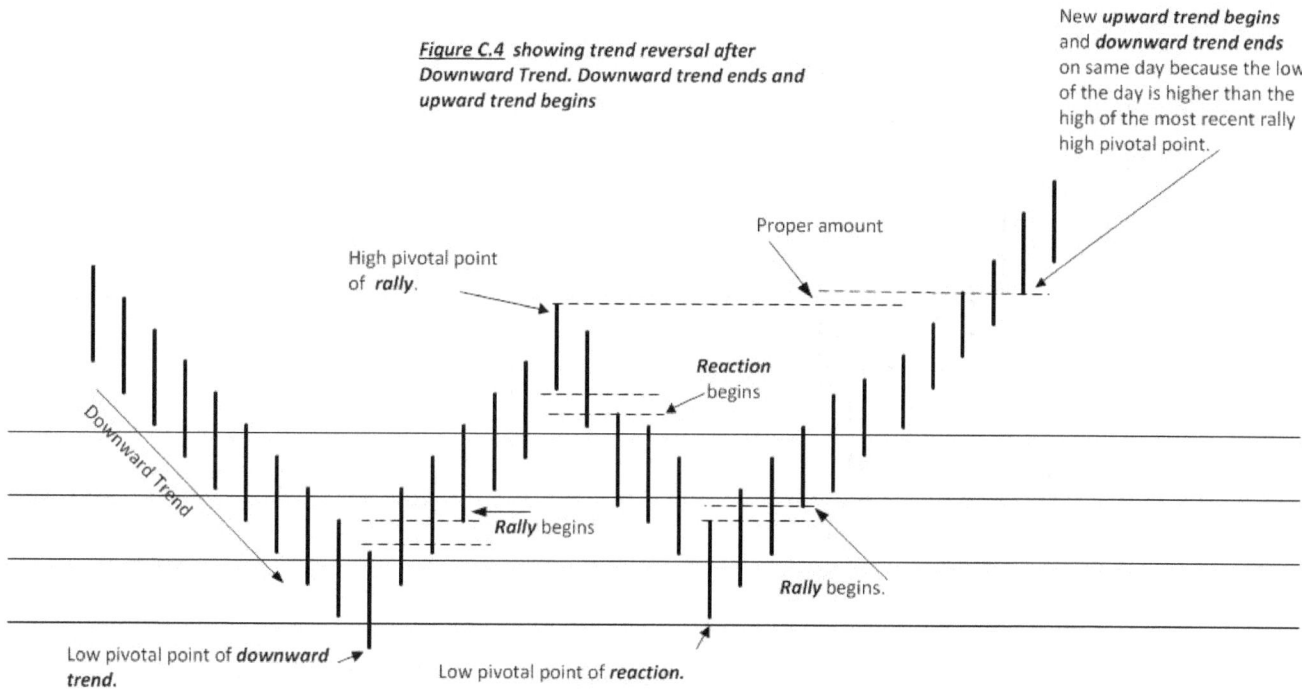

Figure C.4 showing trend reversal after Downward Trend. Downward trend ends and upward trend begins

New **upward trend begins** and **downward trend ends** on same day because the low of the day is higher than the high of the most recent rally high pivotal point.

Proper amount

High pivotal point of **rally**.

Reaction begins

Downward Trend

Rally begins

Rally begins.

Low pivotal point of **downward** trend.

Low pivotal point of **reaction**.

Fig C.4
New Chapt 3

In Figures C.3 and C.4 above, we see the reversal of trend after only one rally or reaction. However, there can be more than one rally or reaction following the pivotal point of a trend, in fact there usually is. ***But when we are looking at the reversal of a trend, the most important pivotal point is the one formed by the most recent rally or reaction.*** Figures C.5 and C.6 below show a trend reversal after several rallies and reactions

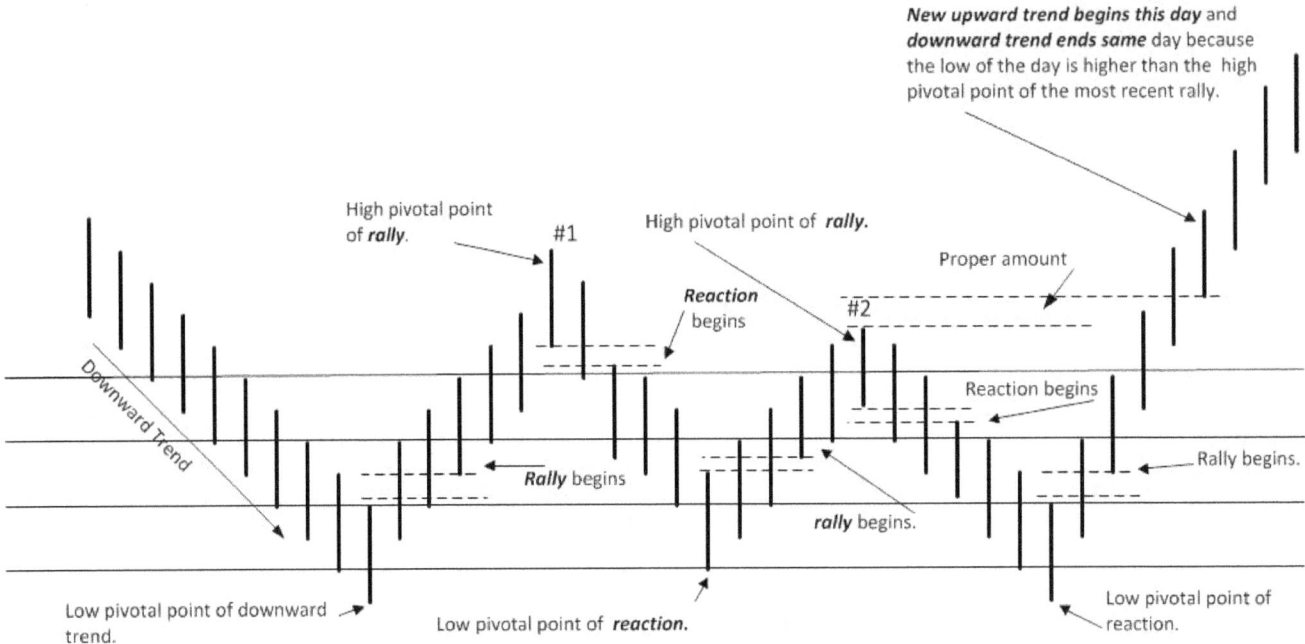

Figure C.5 showing trend reversal from downward trend to upward trend after several rallies & reactions.

New upward trend begins this day and **downward trend ends same** day because the low of the day is higher than the high pivotal point of the most recent rally.

High pivotal point of *rally*.

#1

High pivotal point of *rally.*

Reaction begins

#2

Proper amount

Downward Trend

Reaction begins

Rally begins.

Rally begins

rally begins.

Rally begins.

Low pivotal point of downward trend.

Low pivotal point of *reaction.*

Low pivotal point of reaction.

Fig C.5 New
Chapt 3

Notice in Figure C.5 above that pivotal point #2 is lower than pivotal point #1. Yet it is the piercing of the pivotal point #2 by the proper amount that signals the beginning of the new upward trend. The reason for this is that the actual *price* itself *is not important*. What is important is that it is a ***pivotal point*** and it is the ***most recent*** pivotal point and that it was pierced by the proper amount.

The same applies to the reaction pivotal points #1 and #2 in Figure C.6 below. Pivotal point #2 is not lower than pivotal point #1 yet it is the piercing of pivotal point #2 by the proper amount that signals the beginning of the new downward trend. The reason for this is that the actual *price* itself *is not important*. What is important is that it is a ***pivotal point*** and it is the ***most recent*** pivotal point and that it was pierced by the proper amount.

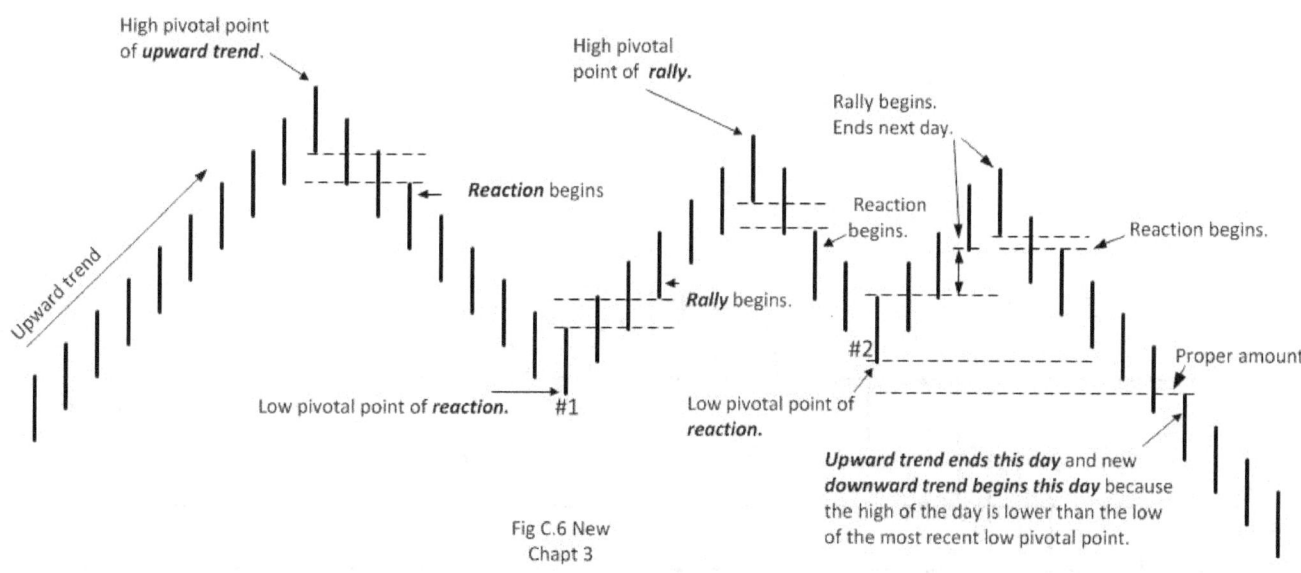

Figure C.6 *showing trend reversal from upward trend to downward trend after several rallies & reactions.*

Fig C.6 New
Chapt 3

27

The following are a few more points to consider regarding rallies and reactions:

1) Rallies and reactions occur only when the price is moving in the opposite direction of the previous pivotal point. Figure Z5 below shows a stock in a rally or upward trend which then experiences a reaction. Notice that the reaction continues and the high of the day is eventually lower than the low of a prior day. ***This does not signal anything and should not be viewed as any type of signal. It is simply a powerful reaction that is cascading downward. Until it crosses a previous pivotal point, this movement remains a reaction only.***

Figure Z5 *showing a reaction that does not cross a pivotal point does not signal anything.*

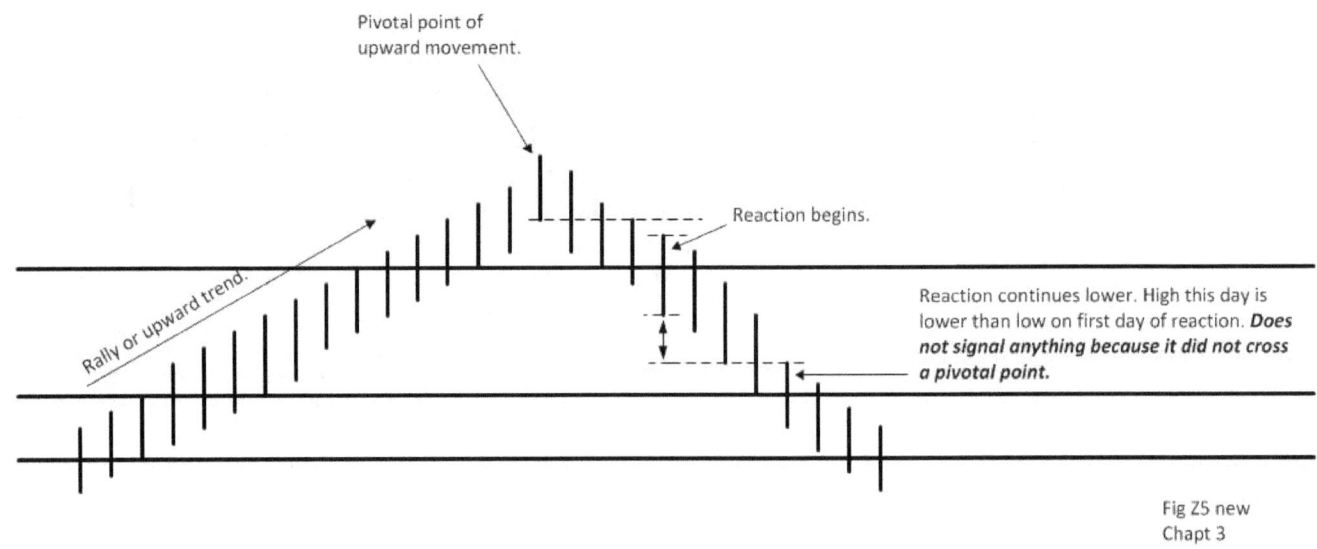

Pivotal point of upward movement.

Reaction begins.

Rally or upward trend.

Reaction continues lower. High this day is lower than low on first day of reaction. ***Does not signal anything because it did not cross a pivotal point.***

Fig Z5 new
Chapt 3

Figure Z6 below shows the same principle applies to rallies after reaction or downward trends.

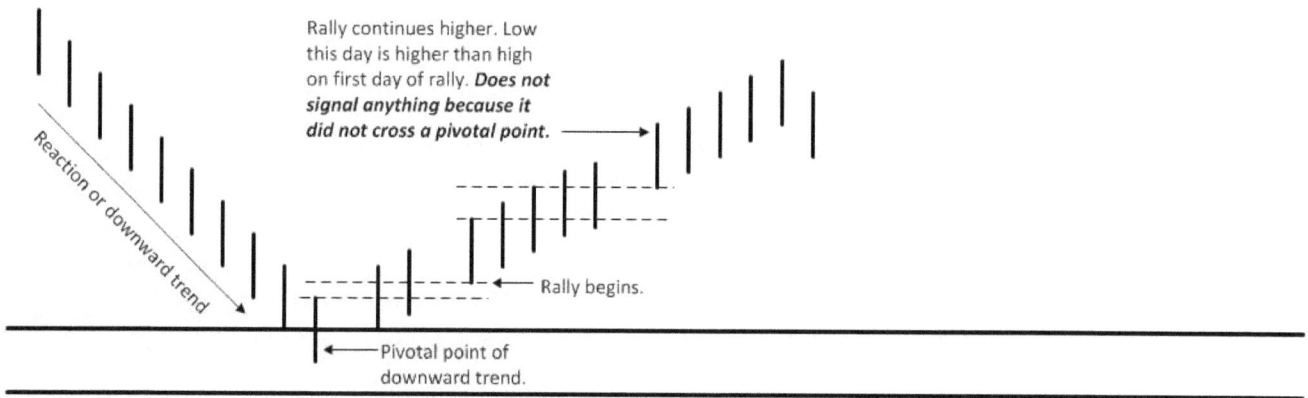

Figure Z6 *showing a rally that does not cross a pivotal point does not signal anything.*

Rally continues higher. Low this day is higher than high on first day of rally. ***Does not signal anything because it did not cross a pivotal point.*** ⟶

Reaction or downward trend

⟵ Rally begins.

⟵ Pivotal point of downward trend.

2) Figure C1 below shows a stock in an upward trend which reaches its highest point then experiences a *reaction*. Figure C1 shows how this stock *remains in an upward trend and is experiencing only a reaction.* It then drifts along with no rally or reaction. Because it has not rallied and crossed the high pivotal point of the trend, nor has it crossed the low pivotal point of *reaction* it remains in an upward trend.

Figure C1 *showing an upward trend and reaction with no change in trend.*

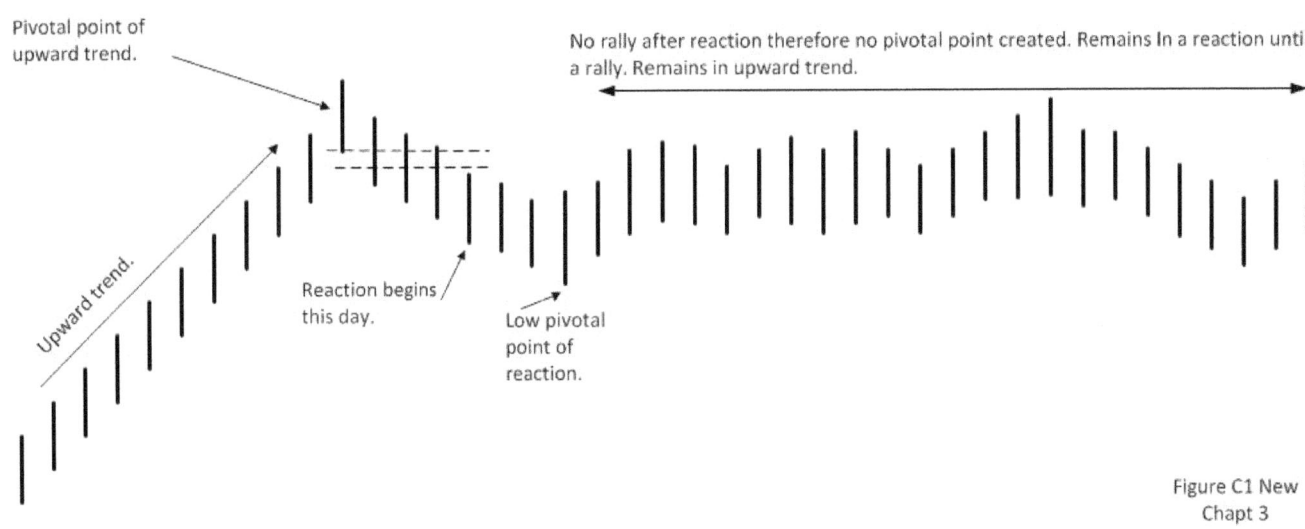

This stock is simply drifting along. *Price action is not creating any rally or reaction and therefore no pivotal point(s).* That means *it remains in an upward trend and is experiencing only a reaction* until it crosses either the last upper or lower pivotal point by the proper amount or creates a new pivotal point and crosses it.

No rally after reaction therefore no pivotal point created. Remains In a reaction until a rally. Remains in upward trend.

Pivotal point of upward trend.

Upward trend.

Reaction begins this day.

Low pivotal point of reaction.

Figure C1 New
Chapt 3

30

Figure C2 below shows a stock in a downward trend which reaches its lowest point then experiences a *rally*. Figure C2 shows how this stock *remains in a downward trend and is experiencing only a rally.* It then drifts along with no rally or reaction. Because it has not had another reaction and crossed the low pivotal point of the trend, nor has it crossed the high pivotal point of the *rally* it remains in a downward trend.

Figure C2 showing a downward trend and rally with no change in trend.

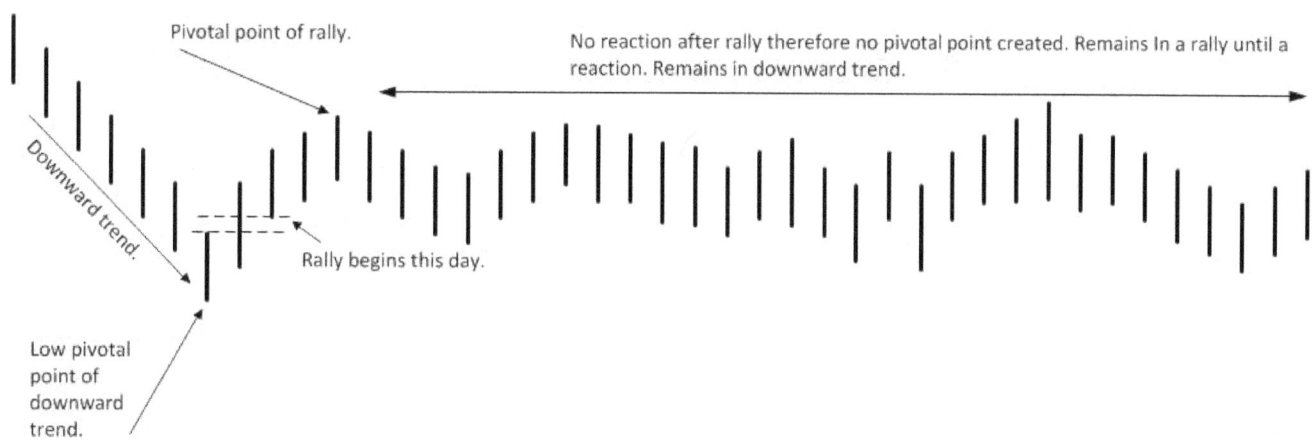

This stock is simply drifting along. **Price action is not creating any rally or reaction and therefore no pivotal point(s).** That means it remains in an downward trend and is experiencing only a rally until it crosses either the last upper or lower pivotal point by the proper amount or creates a new pivotal point and crosses it.

Pivotal point of rally.

No reaction after rally therefore no pivotal point created. Remains In a rally until a reaction. Remains in downward trend.

Downward trend.

Rally begins this day.

Low pivotal point of downward trend.

Figure C2 New
Chapt 3

As can be seen from Figures C1 and C2 a trend remains unchanged even though it experiences a rally or reaction or several rallies and reactions. As stated earlier, in order for a trend to either continue its present trend or to reverse its trend it must break through *the most recent pivotal point.*

These smaller movements are nothing more than the daily oscillation of prices that goes on each day as the result of the battle between buyers and sellers. As we have seen, these daily fluctuations are important to us because eventually they form rallies, reactions, pivotal points and trends.

CHAPTER 3

The Three Critical Rallies and Reactions

Whenever a stock is in a trend and begins to experience rallies or reactions there is a specific order in which these rallies and reactions occur that helps us form an opinion as to whether the current trend has ended or if it will continue. In order to simplify the identification of those rallies and reactions they have been given names. In the case of a ***downward trend*** their names and order are:

1) First Rally

2) ***Follow up reaction***

3) Buy Rally

In the case of an ***upward trend*** their names and order are:

1) First Reaction

2) ***Follow up rally***

3) Sell Reaction

The two most important of these above movements are the follow up rally and the follow up reaction.

In this chapter we will learn how to use the ***pivotal points of trends*** to recognize the first rally or reaction, the ***follow up rally*** or reaction and the ***buy or sell rally or reaction***.

When a stock is in a *trend* and a rally or reaction occurs, that very first rally or reaction is referred to as the *first rally* or *first reaction*. The rally or reaction following the first rally or first reaction is referred to as the *follow up rally* or *follow up reaction*. The rally or reaction that follows the *follow up rally* or reaction is the *buy rally* or the *sell reaction*. Keep in mind that multiple *first rallies, first reactions, follow up rallies and reactions, buy rallies* and *sell reactions* can occur throughout the course of a large trend.

For example, Figure CA shows a stock in an upward trend which experiences a *first reaction* followed by a *follow up rally*. The *follow up rally* pierces the upward trend pivotal point by the proper amount so the upward trend continues. It is because the upward trend continued higher that several days later the upward trend experiences another *first reaction* and another *follow up rally*.

Figure CA showing multiple first reactions and follow up rallies within an upward trend.

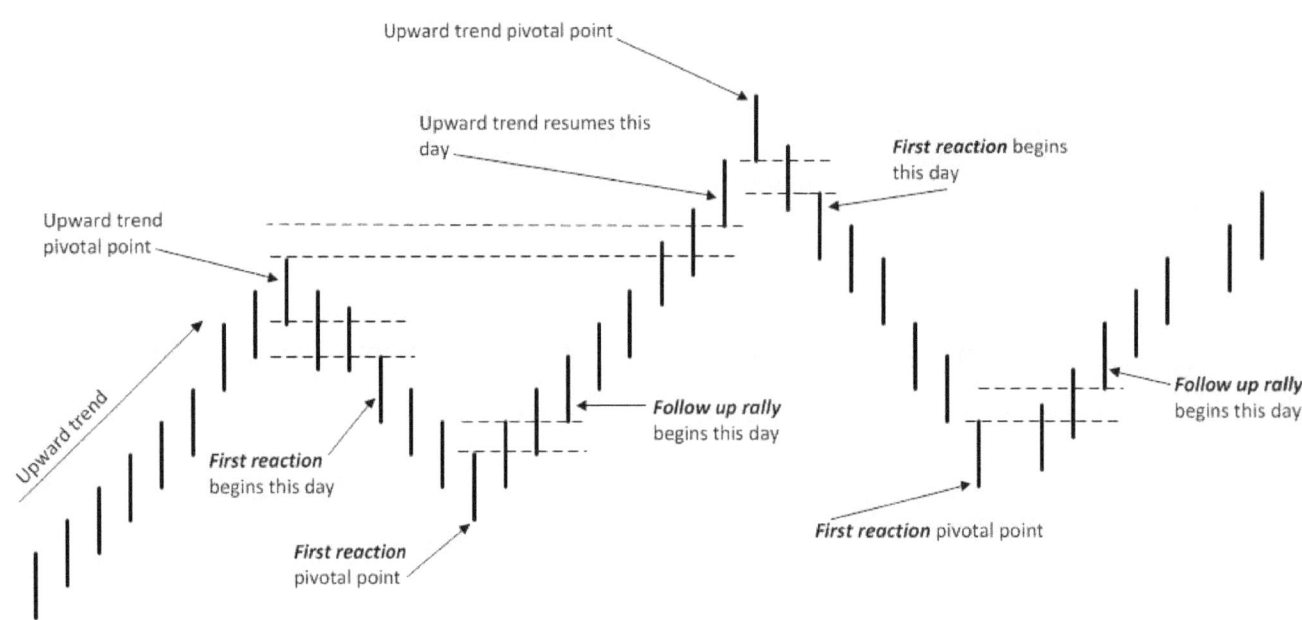

34

In Figure CA above if the *follow up rally* had not pierced the upward trend pivotal point by the proper amount and a reaction occurred that reaction would now be the *sell reaction*. See Figure Z1 below.

As we can see in Figure Z1, the upward trend reaches it high pivotal point and experienced a *first reaction*. That *first reaction* was followed by a *follow up rally*. The *follow up rally* failed to pierce the previous high pivotal point and a *sell reaction* followed. *It is on the first day of that sell reaction that we recognize that the upward trend is probably over.*

Figure Z1 showing follow up rally does not pierce upward trend pivotal point by proper amount. Reaction follows indicating upward trend is over.

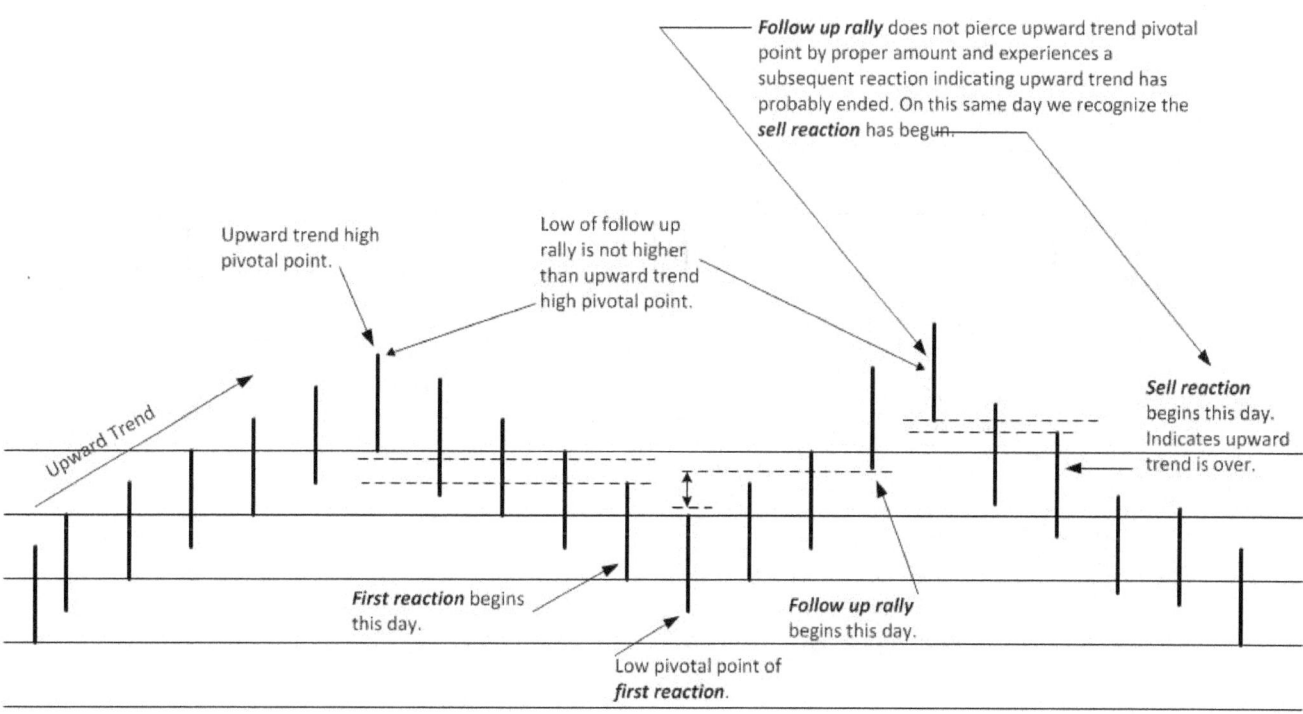

Fig Z1 New Chapt 3

The same applies to Figure Z2 below which shows a downward trend which reached its low pivotal point and experienced a *first rally*. That *first rally* was followed by a *follow up reaction*. That *follow up reaction* failed to pierce the previous low pivotal point and a *buy rally* followed it. *It is on the first day of that buy rally that we recognize the downward trend has probably ended.*

Figure Z2 showing follow up reaction does not pierce downward trend pivotal point by proper amount. Rally follows indicating downward trend is over.

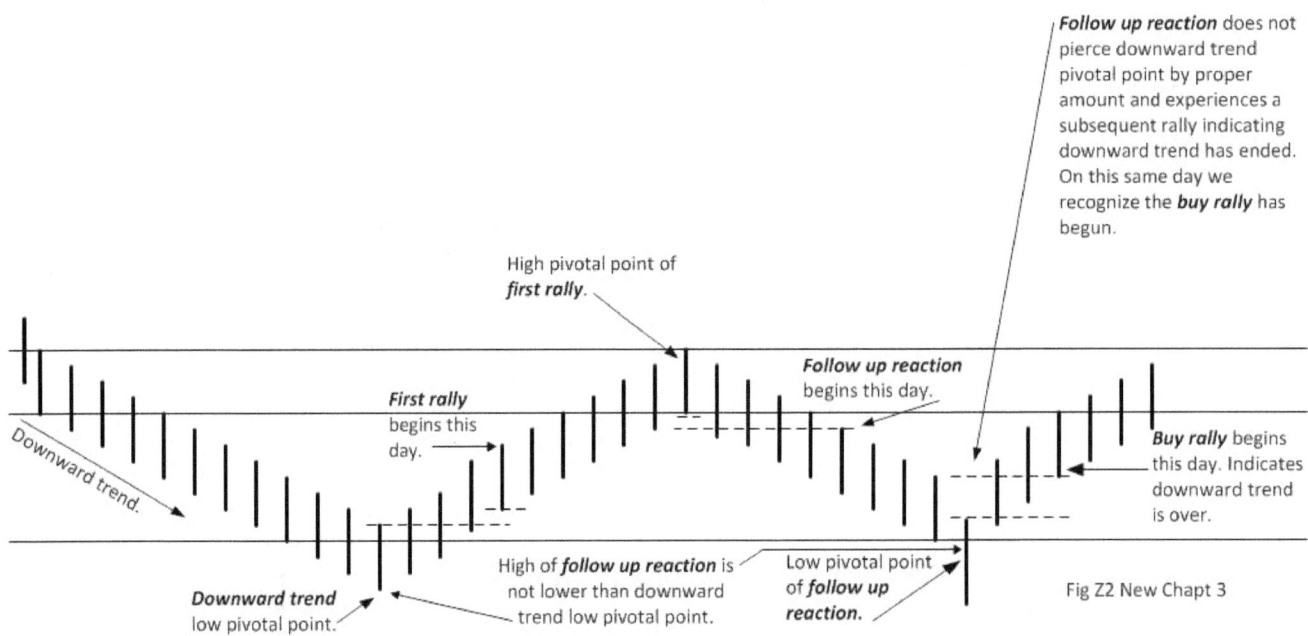

CHAPTER 4

Buying and Selling: The Buy Rally & the Sell Reaction

As stated in Chapter 4 *the two most important movements are the follow up rally and the follow up reaction.* The reason these two movements are of particular importance is because the *follow up rally* and *follow up reaction* are either going to break through the trend pivotal point *by the proper amount* and resume that trend or they will stop short and may eventually produce the *buy rally* or *sell reaction*.

More on the Buy rally and Sell reaction.

The buy rally and sell reaction have those names because that is exactly what they are. The first day of the buy rally or sell reaction is earliest possible point when we recognize that the trend has *probably* ended. They are also the earliest *possible* buy, sell or short sell points at the earliest point of what *may* be the beginning of a new trend. *The very first day of the buy rally or sell reaction is the earliest point at which to place a trade.* But these early buy points are riskier and more nerve racking than if we waited for the day the new trend positively formed by piercing the most recent pivotal point. The formation of the buy rally and the sell reaction occur *before* the positive reversal of trend, see Figures C.7 and C.8. We can see that a few days later the reversal of trend occurs when the first rally or reaction pivotal point has been pierced by the proper amount. Also see Figures C.5 and C.6, Chapter 3.

Figure C.7 showing possible sell & short sell points during trend reversal from Upward Trend to downward trend..

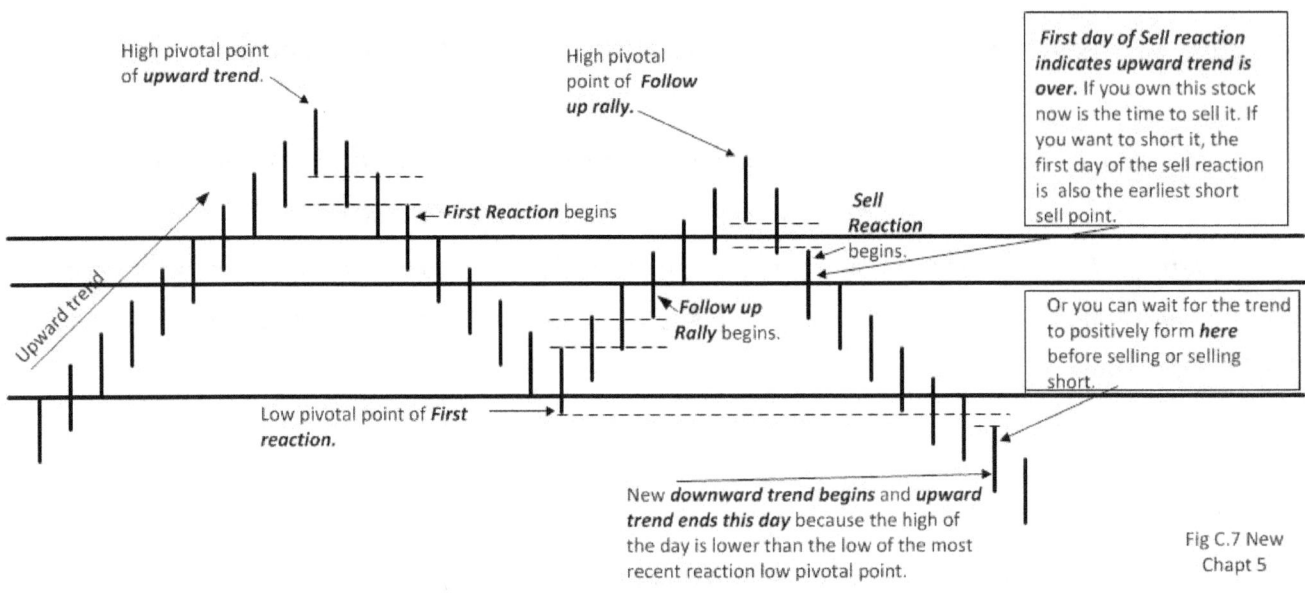

High pivotal point of **upward trend**.

High pivotal point of **Follow up rally.**

← **First Reaction** begins

First day of Sell reaction indicates upward trend is over. If you own this stock now is the time to sell it. If you want to short it, the first day of the sell reaction is also the earliest short sell point.

Sell Reaction begins.

Follow up Rally begins.

Upward trend

Low pivotal point of **First reaction.**

Or you can wait for the trend to positively form **here** before selling or selling short.

New **downward trend begins** and **upward trend ends this day** because the high of the day is lower than the low of the most recent reaction low pivotal point.

Fig C.7 New Chapt 5

Figure C.8 showing possible buy points during trend reversal after Downward Trend. Downward trend ends and upward trend begins

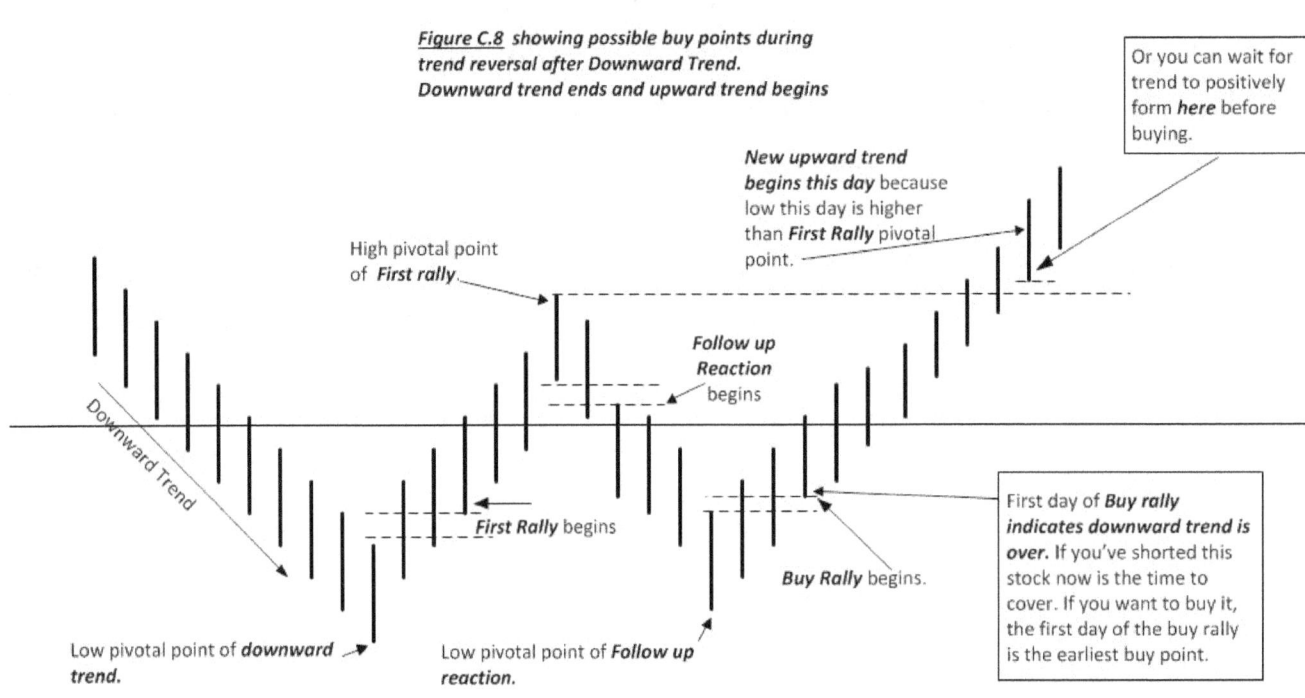

Or you can wait for trend to positively form **here** before buying.

New upward trend begins this day because low this day is higher than **First Rally** pivotal point.

High pivotal point of **First rally.**

Follow up Reaction begins

Downward Trend

First Rally begins

First day of **Buy rally indicates downward trend is over.** If you've shorted this stock now is the time to cover. If you want to buy it, the first day of the buy rally is the earliest buy point.

Buy Rally begins.

Low pivotal point of **downward trend.**

Low pivotal point of **Follow up reaction.**

Fig C.8 New Chapt 5

CHAPTER 5

How Rallies, Reactions and Pivotal Points Are the Ultimate Guides for Protecting Your Profits and Avoiding Big Losses

Now that you are familiar with *The Message Of The Tape* you now have a set of rules and measurements consisting of rallies, reactions, pivotal points and trends. But in the stock market anything can happen and your investment should be watched every day. There is no such thing as a good, safe stock that is as steady as a rock. Stocks simply do not go up or down forever. Even when you heed *The Message Of The Tape* and buy or sell according to Chapter 5, there is no guarantee that your stock will do exactly what you expect it to do or that it will adhere strictly to the rules of *The Message Of The Tape*. In other words, you can be wrong or the *buy rally* or *sell reaction* may not follow through to become a trend, or the stock simply isn't ready to move just yet. Therefore, losses are inevitable.

There are many, many methods on loss avoidance and loss cutting. In his book "How to Trade in Stocks" Jesse Livermore made his exit from a trade at 10% loss, *no exceptions*. Others, like William J. O'Neil in his book "The Successful Investor" advise cutting losses at no more than 7% to 8%, *no exceptions*. What they are saying is no matter how much you love a stock or how much faith and hope you have in its prospects, when your losses amount to around 7% it is time to give up you personal feelings and face the fact that you are losing money. They are also saying that a 7% to 10% loss is better taken now before your loss turns ugly. But they didn't just pick these percentages because they sounded good. It is because after a stock begins to fall beyond 7% to 10% it usually requires an exponentially long time to recover…or it may not recover at all.

They also go on to say that if it does recover you will be given other opportunities in the future to buy it. Those opportunities will not be available to you if you loose all your money by riding it to the bottom.

By using **The Message Of The Tape,** you will find that rallies, reactions and pivotal points are the ultimate guides for protecting your profits and avoiding big losses.

Watch your investment every day. Rallies and reactions are your early warning system.

Let's say that you have read **The Message Of The Tape** and have watched a stock carefully as it has moved steadily in a **downward trend.** Then, it experiences a **first rally**, **follow up reaction** and **buy rally**. These movements caused you to form an opinion that a change of trend is in the making so you bought at the earliest buy point which is on the first day of the buy rally. This stock performed as you thought it would and it eventually pierced the **first rally pivotal point** by the proper amount thereby becoming an **upward trend (figure C.8 chapter 4)**. The upward trend continues for several days. Because you are an alert investor you are watching this stock every day. Then, one day it begins to go down. It keeps going down until one day the **first reaction** is formed. As a result of the **first reaction**, the upward trend pivotal point is established. Because you have read **The Message Of The Tape**, you know exactly what you are looking at. You know that right now your stock remains in an upward trend and is experiencing only a reaction but you also know that that reaction may be an early warning. You are now watching and waiting for the **follow up rally** or further downward movement.

You also know that the ***follow up rally*** is the decisive rally because it **may** continue upward and pierce the upward trend by the proper amount thus resuming the upward trend, or it may stop short and experience a ***sell reaction*** which is the earliest signal that the upward trend may have ended. (See Figures C.5, C.6, C.7, C.8)

Depending on the type of investor you are or how much loss you can tolerate, in the above scenario it is up to you whether you decide to sell on the very first day of the ***first reaction*** or perhaps wait until the ***sell reaction***. If you waited until the ***sell reaction*** you may have lost some profit but you probably would not have lost money unless the upward trend was very shallow, which does happen. By selling on the first day of the ***first reaction*** only a very small amount of profit would have been lost and you would also be in the position to re enter on the day the ***follow up rally*** crossed the upward trend pivotal point.

Other scenarios are also possible. After the first reaction there could be a series of rallies and reactions with no definitive change in trend. This was explained in Chapter 3 and Figures C1 and C2. ***Because you now know what the signals are***, you now have the knowledge to decide whether to exit cautiously preserving your capital and profit or waiting until ***the stock itself*** gives you the definitive signal.

It is important to point out that when using rallies, reactions and pivotal points as your guide, a stock in a trend can experience a rally or reaction that moves more than 7% or 10%. But knowing that for the time being that your stock is in a definite trend and is experiencing only a rally or reaction enables you to make an informed decision whether to hold that stock until the next movement or to exit.

CHAPTER 6

-Observe it before You Buy it-
Get to Know Your Stock Using Rallies & Reactions

"Stocks, like individuals, have character and personality. Some are high-strung, nervous, and jumpy; others are forthright, direct, logical".

Jesse Livermore

What Jesse Livermore said is true. Stocks have personalities. That's why it is important to observe your stock for a while in order to get to know its personality. The best way to do that is by using rallies and reactions.

So far, for the purpose of illustration, all of the figures in this book have shown a "stock" that is forthright, direct, logical. Figure 7.1 below shows a real stock that is "high strung, nervous and jumpy".

Fig 7.1 *Example of " high strung, nervous and jumpy" stock.*

Volume (millions)   SMA(15)

Thank you ETRADE

Figure 7.2 below shows a stock that is "forthright, direct, logical."

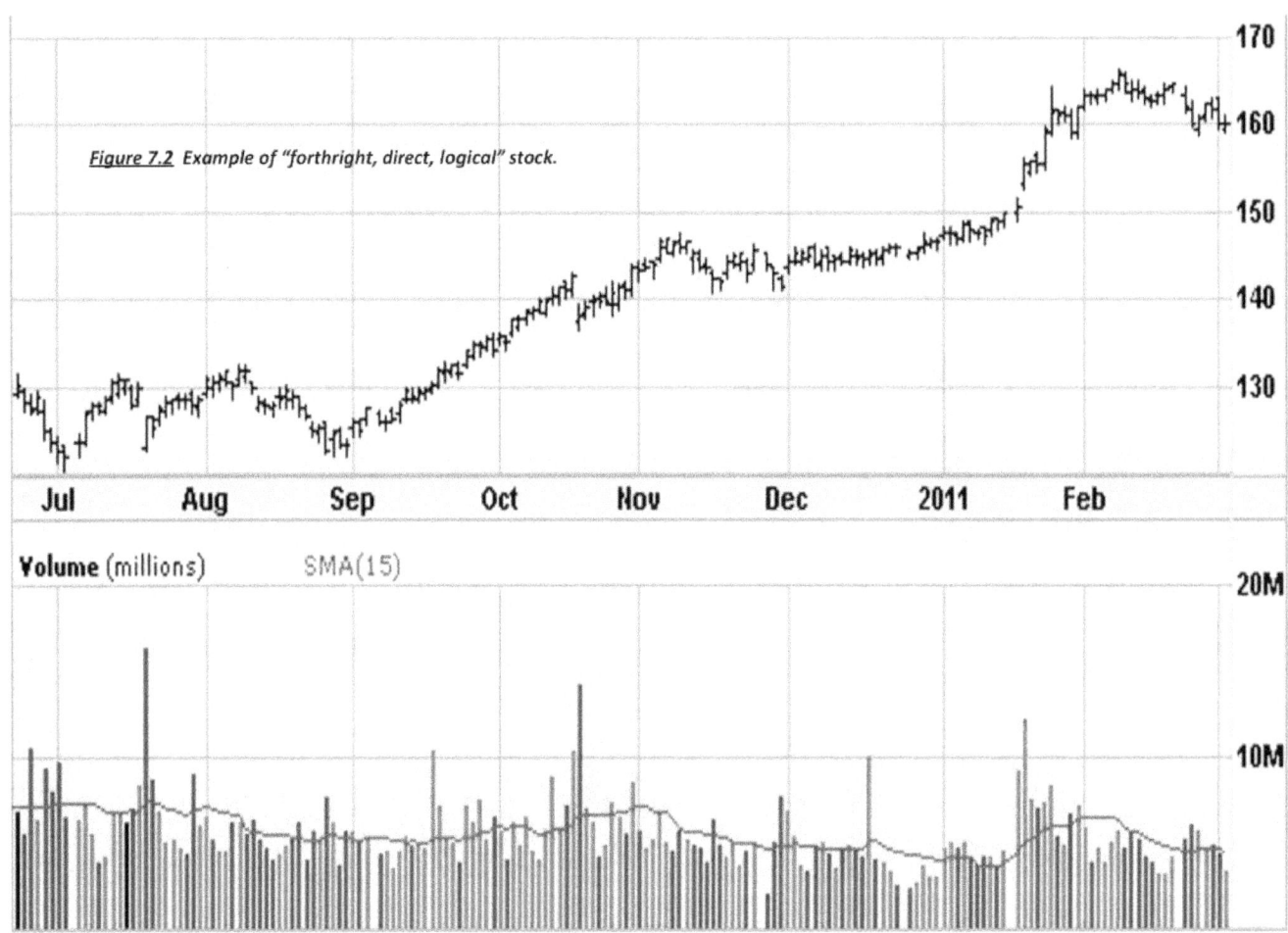

Figure 7.2 Example of "forthright, direct, logical" stock.

Very little needs to be said about the stock in Figure 7.2. Figure 7.1 is a different story. Figure 7.1 would be referred to today as a volatile stock. It is the nervous stock in Figure 7.1 where the measurement system in this book can help you the most. This stock is moving fairly rapidly between trends in volatile, large spreads. But by using *The Message Of The Tape* you have a clear warning system, -that is rallies, reactions and pivotal points- to help warn you of possible surprises.

The False Rally or Reaction

In Figure 7.3 below we see the formation of a *false rally*. False rallies or reactions occur whenever there is a price spike off *any* pivotal point regardless if it's a rally, reaction or trend pivotal point. In Figure 7.3 we see the high price moves extremely high but the low is not higher than the high price on the day the downward trend reached its lowest point. Therefore, ***no rally or downward trend pivotal point is formed***. As we already have learned, this stock remains in a downward trend. We also observe that several days later the lows of the day are high enough to create a *first rally* but their highs are not higher than the high of the *price spike*. For this reason no rally is created and this stock remains in a downward trend.

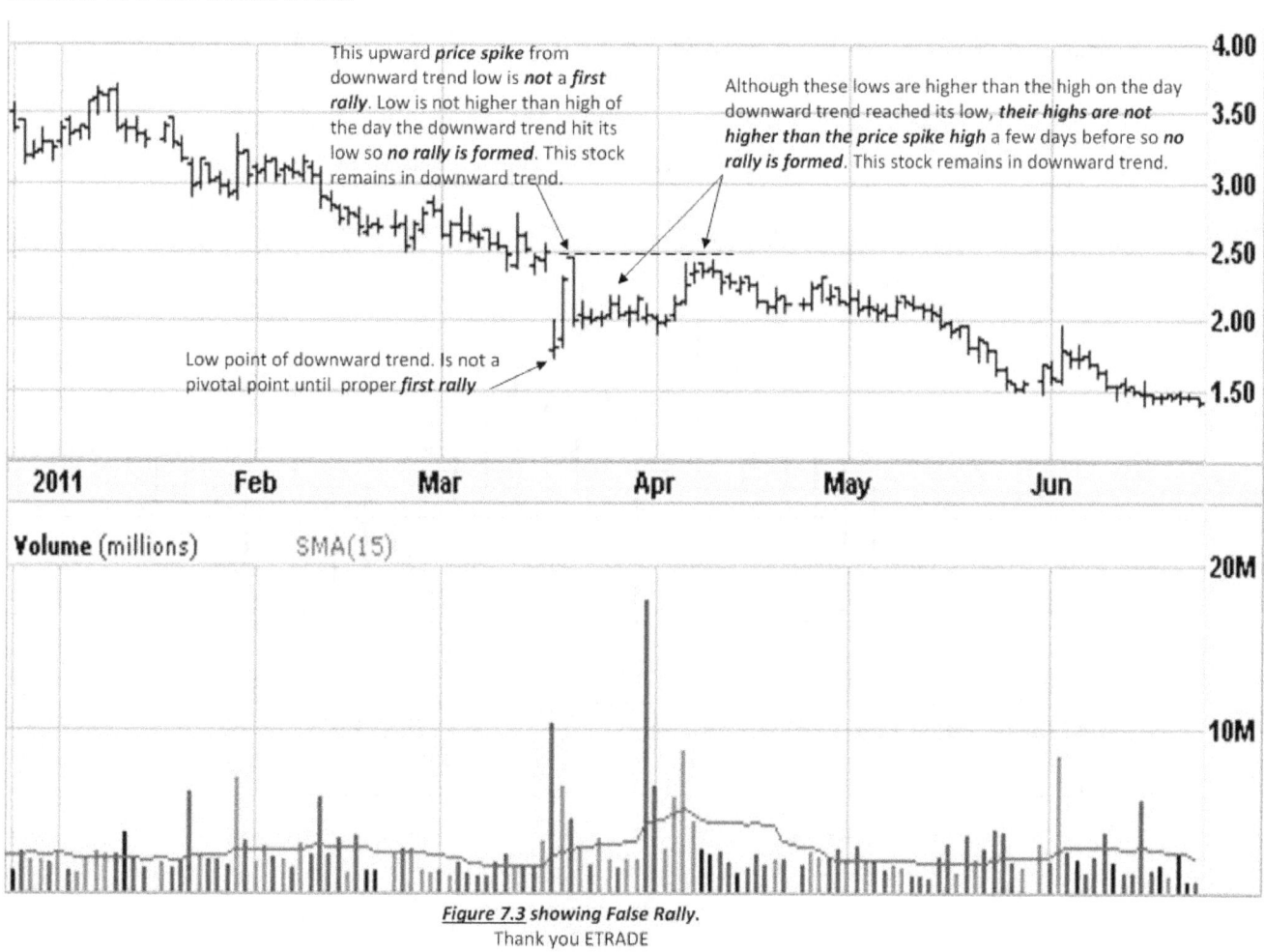

Figure 7.3 showing False Rally.
Thank you ETRADE

In Figure 7.4 below we see the formation of a *false reaction*. False rallies or reactions occur whenever there is a price spike off *any* pivotal point regardless if it's a rally, reaction or trend pivotal point. In Figure 7.4 we see the low price moves extremely low but the high is not lower than the low price on the day the upward trend reached its highest point. ***Therefore, no reaction or upward trend pivotal point is formed***. As we already have learned, this stock remains in an upward trend. We also observe that several days later the highs of the day are low enough to create a *first reaction* but their lows are not lower than the low of the price spike. For this reason no reaction is created and this stock remains in an upward trend.

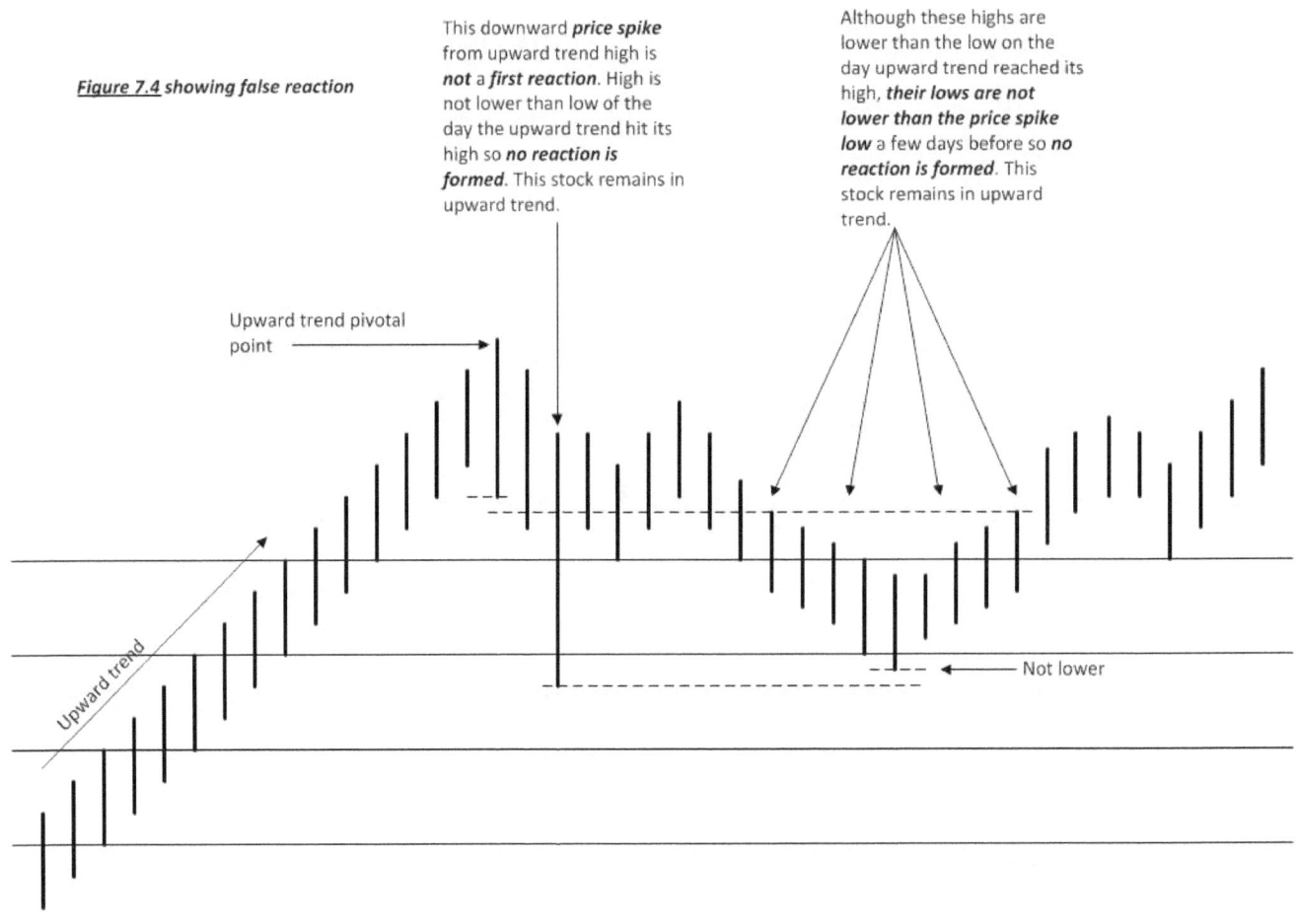

Figure 7.4 showing false reaction

This downward *price spike* from upward trend high is *not a first reaction*. High is not lower than low of the day the upward trend hit its high so *no reaction is formed*. This stock remains in upward trend.

Although these highs are lower than the low on the day upward trend reached its high, *their lows are not lower than the price spike low* a few days before so *no reaction is formed*. This stock remains in upward trend.

Upward trend pivotal point

Upward trend

Not lower

CHAPTER 7

Let's Have a Look at the DOW

Wouldn't it have been good to know back in October of 2007 immediately after the Dow hit its highest high ever of over 14,000, that it immediately began giving signals that the overall market was softening and perhaps forming a downward trend?

Wouldn't it have been good to know back in mid 2008 that the downward trend that began in late 2007 was actually resuming and that the Dow was giving signals that the overall market was heading down even further? It eventually reached a low below 6,500.

The answer to these two questions is obvious.

We can see in Figure 8.2 below that the downward trend that began in November of 2007, *less than one month after reaching its all time high*, continued with only intermittent recovery until it reached its low of about 6,500 in early 2009.

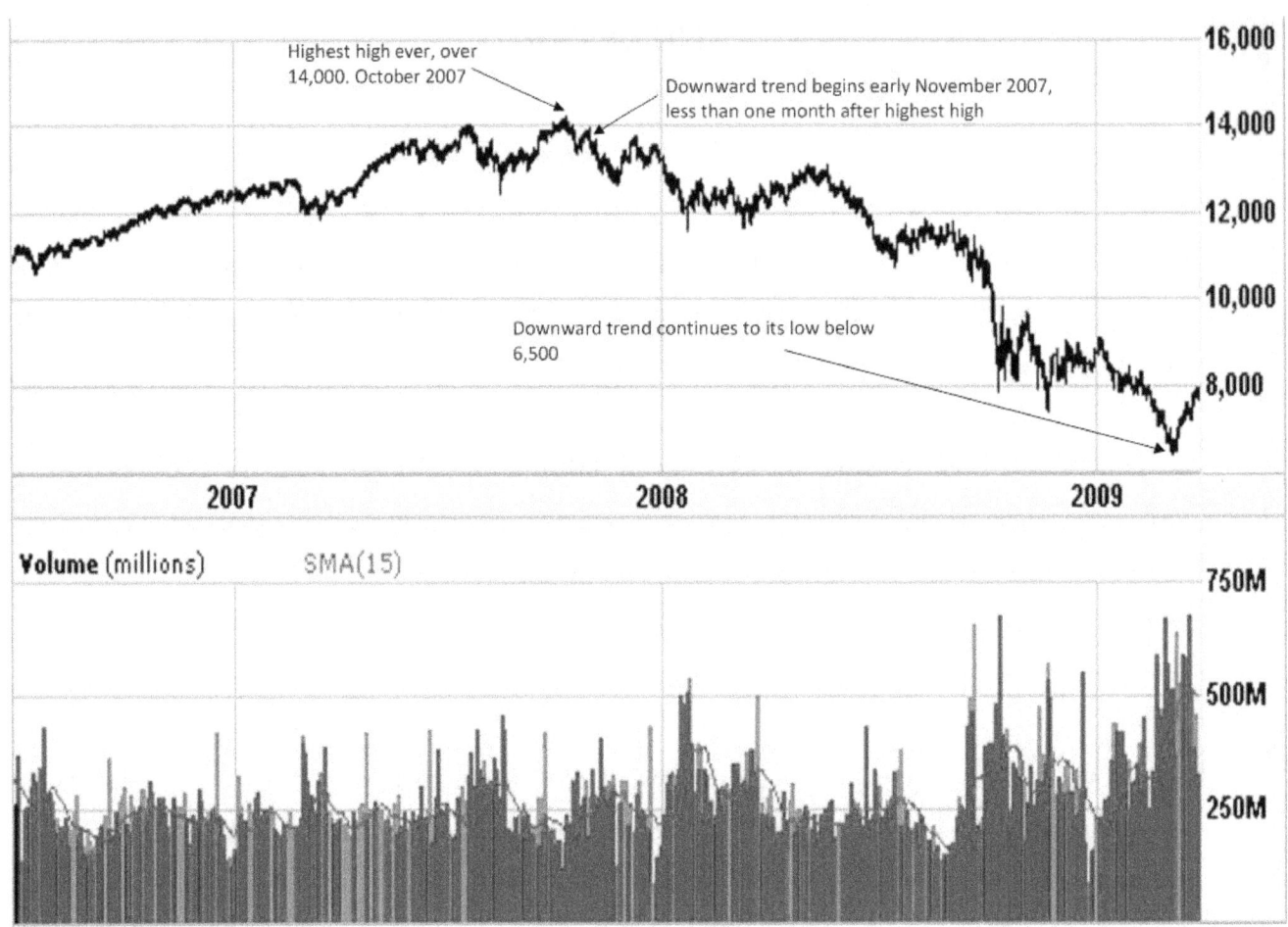

Figure 8.2 *DJIA Sept 2007 to March 2009*
Thank you ETRADE

As stated in Chapter 1, *The Message Of The Tape* is applicable to all commodities, currencies, indices, index funds, mutual funds, exchange traded funds (ETF) and preferred stocks. Because the action of any stock is tied to the action of the overall market, it is important to keep an eye on the overall market as well.

So, let us have a look at the Dow Jones Industrial Average (DJIA) during that incredible time from October 2007 when it hit its highest high ever to February 2008 to see how *The Message Of The Tape* could have helped us.

Looking at Figure 8.1 below we can see how the action of rallies, reactions and pivotal points gives us ample information that the overall market, which is represented by the DJIA, was becoming soft and that a change of trend was in the making.

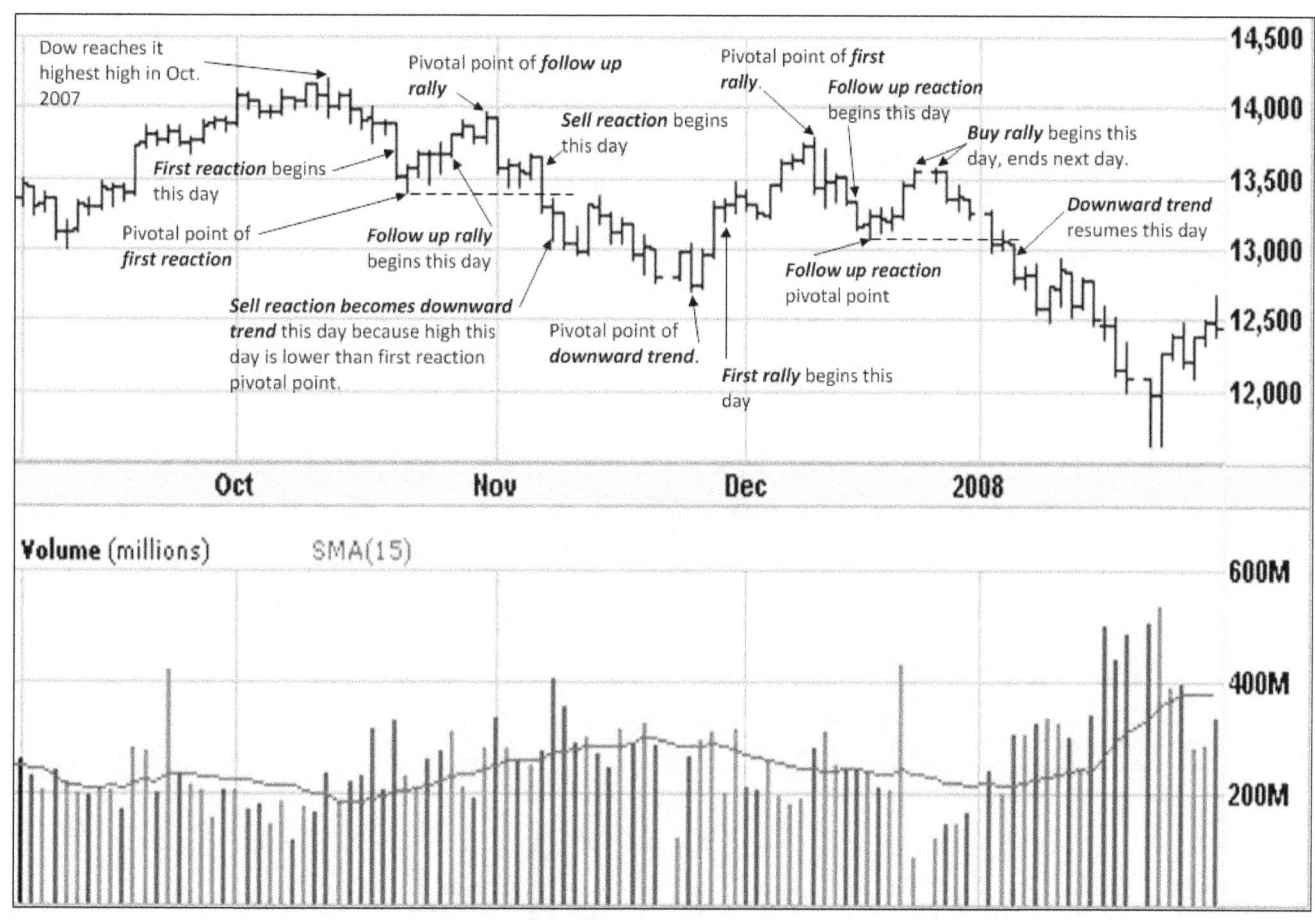

Figure 8.1 Dow Jones Industrial Average Daily September 2007 to February 2008.
Thank you ETRADE

By understanding *The Message Of The Tape* we would have been able to easily identify the warning signs that the overall market was softening as illustrated in Figure 8.1 above. *The DJIA began a downward trend that began in early November of 2007 which is less than one month after reaching it highest point ever.*

CHAPTER 8

Examples of The Message Of The Tape Applied to Real Stocks

Figure 9.1 below is a chart of Microsoft which was clearly in a downward trend from early 2008 into the first quarter of 2009. You can see in early March 2009 the downward trend reached its low and Microsoft reversed its trend from downward to upward

Figure 9.1 showing Trend reversal Microsoft (MSFT) January 2008 – January 2010
Thank you ETRADE

On the above chart we don't see the daily details of what occurred during the critical period of late February to mid March 2009 when Microsoft reversed its trend from downward to upward. Figure 9.2 is the detail daily chart of that critical period.

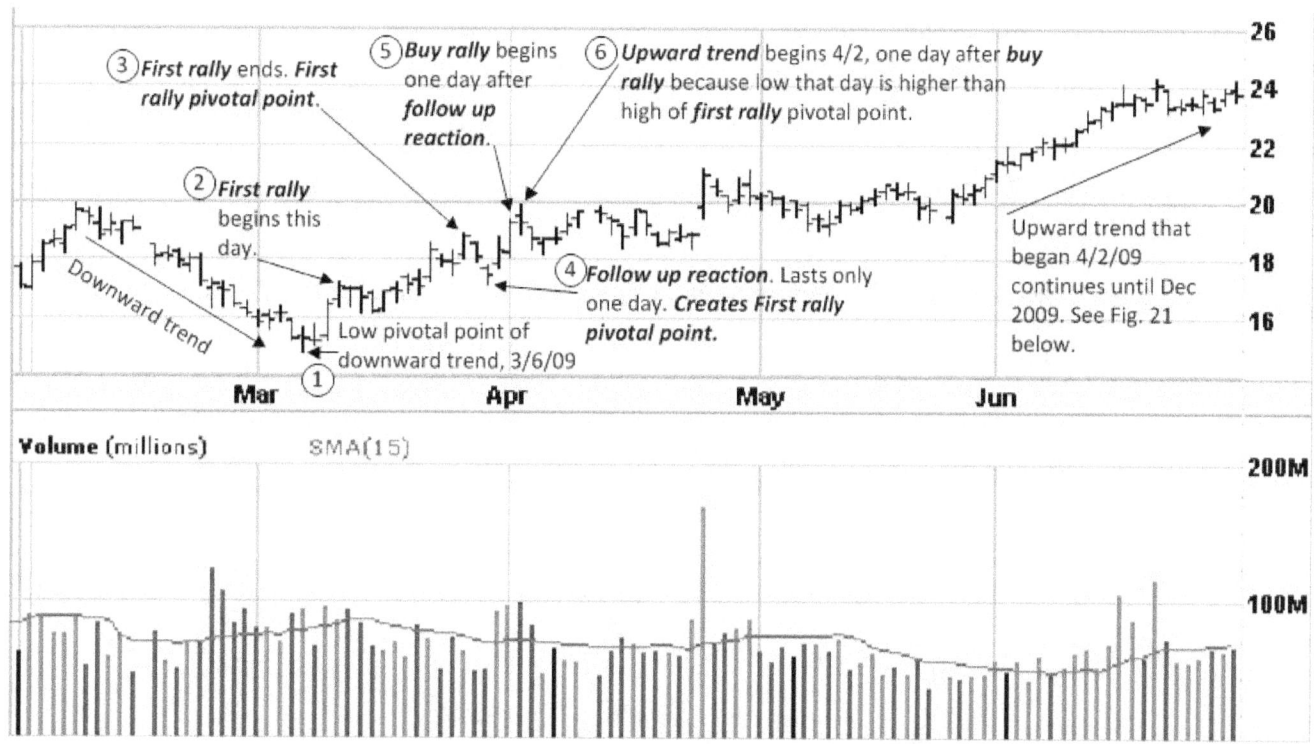

Figure 9.2 showing details of trend reversal. Microsoft
(Msft) early 2009. Thank you ETRADE

We see in Figure 9.2 above that on March 6th Microsoft reached its low of $14.87 (1). The high price that day was $15.62. On March 9th, we see the prices begin to move upward which continues to March 11th. On March 11th, we recognize that the ***first rally*** is in the making because the low on March 11th of $16.43 is higher than the high of $15.62 on March 6th, the lowest point of the downward trend which began in early 2008 (2).

This ***first rally*** continues without a reaction until it reaches its extreme high of $18.88 on March 26th. Low that day was $18.12 (3).

On March 30th, we recognize a ***follow up reaction*** is in the making because the high that day of $17.76 is lower than the low of $18.12 on March 26th the day the ***first rally*** made its high (4). On March 31st, we recognize that the ***buy rally*** is in the making because the low that day of $17.78 is higher than the March 30th high of $17.76 which is the day the ***follow up reaction*** reached its low (5).

On April 2nd, we recognize the beginning of an upward trend because the low that day of $19.00 *is higher than the high of the first rally* which reached its high of $18.88 on March 26th (6).

As you can see by Figure 9.3 below, the upward trend that began April 2nd continued until late 2009.

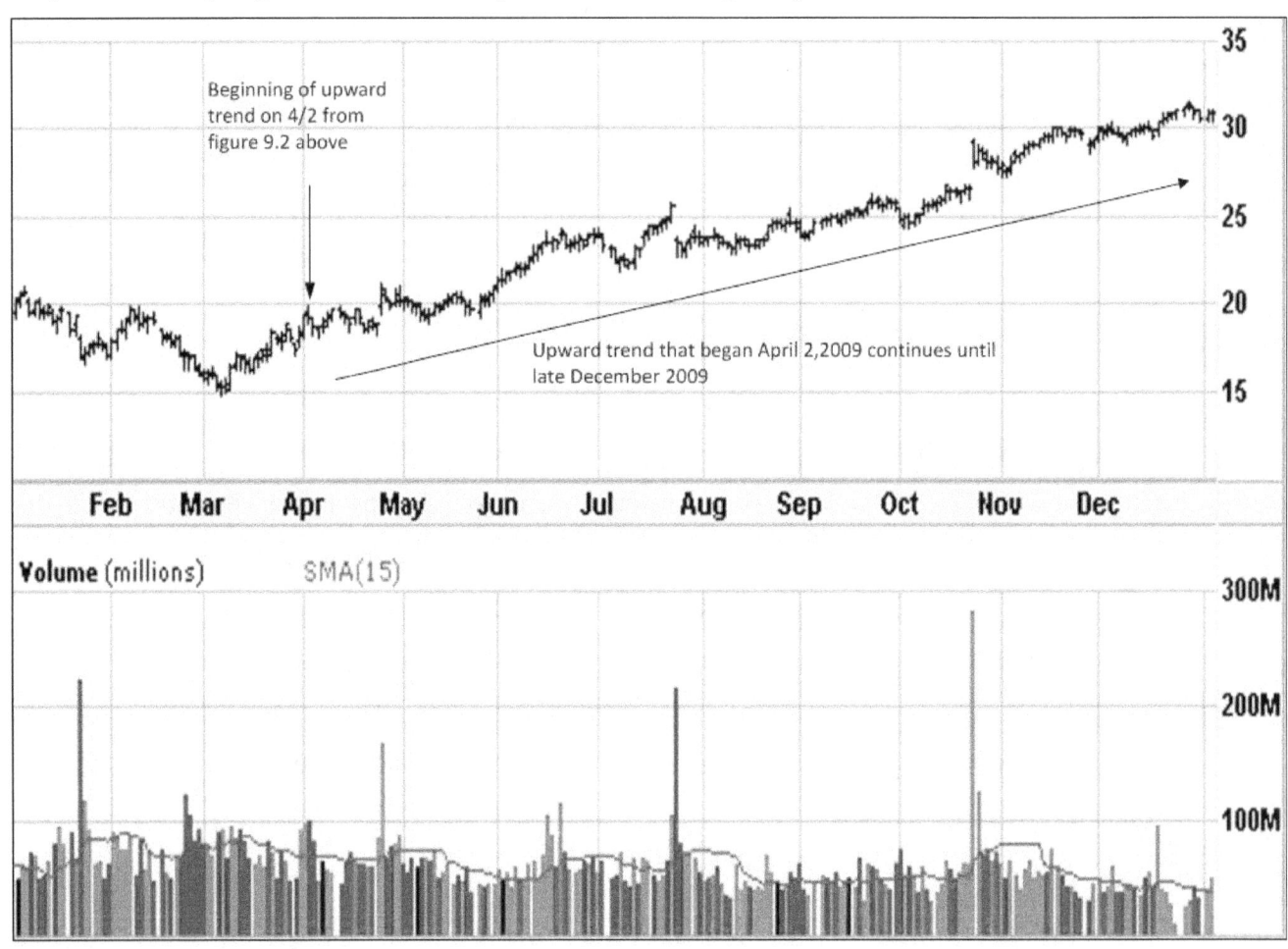

Beginning of upward trend on 4/2 from figure 9.2 above

Upward trend that began April 2,2009 continues until late December 2009

Volume (millions)   SMA(15)

Figure 9.3 showing upward trend begins 4/2/09 and continues until 12/09. Thank you ETRADE

Diagram 9.4 below shows a typical daily OHCL chart of Microsoft (MSFT) for the period of 4/2010 to 4/2011. As can be seen from the chart Diagram 9.4 below, Microsoft was in a steep downward trend from late April 2010 through July 1, 2010.

Figure 9.4 showing Microsoft (MSFT) steep downward trend and later upward trend during 2010
Thank you ETRADE

In Figure 9.5 below, we zoomed in to get a more detailed look at Microsoft during the critical time around July 1ˢᵗ 2010 when it **may** have been signaling the end of that steep downward trend.

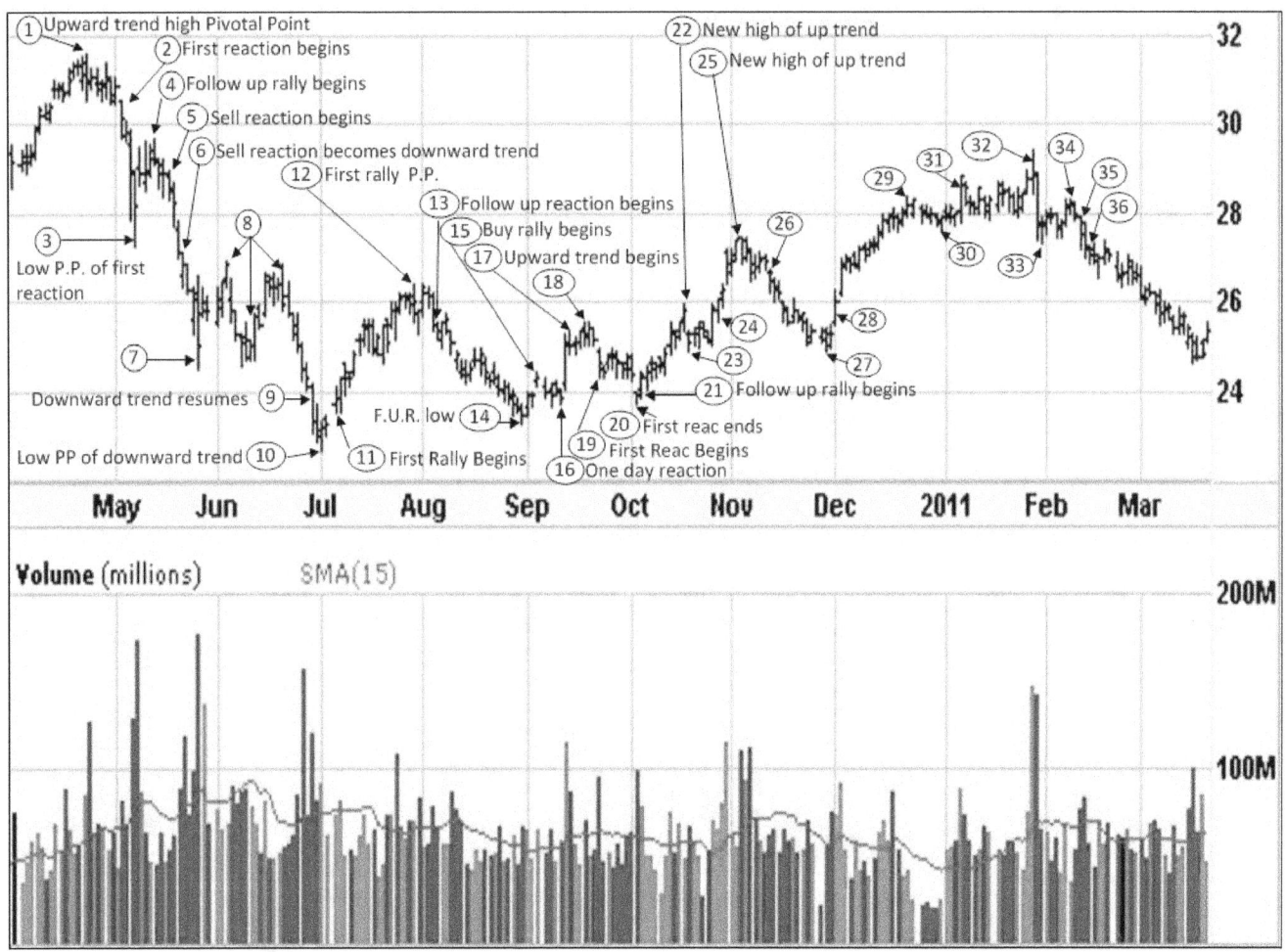

Figure 9.5 MSFT - June 1 –Oct 2010   Thank you Etrade

In Figure 9.5 above, we see that Microsoft was in an upward trend until April 23ʳᵈ (1). High that day was \$31.58. The low was \$30.65. A **first reaction** began on May 4ᵗʰ because the high that day was lower than the low of April 23ʳᵈ (2). The **first reaction** continues until its low of \$27.30 on May 7ᵗʰ, the high on May 7ᵗʰ was \$28.95 (3). A one day **follow up rally** began on May 13ᵗʰ because the low of \$29.18 is higher than the high on May 7ᵗʰ (4) (3). On May 18ᵗʰ **a sell reaction** began because the high that day was lower than the low on May 13ᵗʰ (5).

The **sell reaction** continues downward until May 21st when it becomes a downward trend because the high on May 21st is lower than the low of the ***first reaction*** (6) (3). The downward trend continues to an initial low of $24.56 on May 26th (7). The high on May 26th was $26.61. From May 26th to June 21st no rallies or reactions are created so this stock remains in a downward trend (8). However, on June 29th the high was lower than the low of $24.56 on May 26th (7) so the downward trend resumed (7) (9). The downward trend continues until July 1st when it reaches a low of $22.73 (10).

On July 2nd the price begins to move upwards away from the downtrend low of $22.73. On July 6th we recognize that a ***first rally*** is in the making because the low that day of $23.58 is higher than the high of $23.32 on July 1st, the lowest point of the downward trend (11).

We observe that this ***first rally*** which began on July 6th continues without reaction until July 29th when it reaches its high of $26.41. Low that day was $25.60 (12).

On August 5th we recognize that **the follow up reaction** is in the making because the high that day of $25.58 is lower than the low of $25.60 on July 29th the day the ***first rally*** reached its high (13).

This **follow up reaction** that began on August 5th continued without a rally until it hit its low price of $23.32 on August 31st (14). High that day was $23.73.

On September 1ˢᵗ the price changed direction and a normal upward movement began in response to the August 31ˢᵗ low. We see that the prices continue to climb on September 2ⁿᵈ and 3ʳᵈ. On September 3ʳᵈ we recognize that a *first rally* is in the making because September 3ʳᵈ is the first day that the low of $24.45 is higher than the high of $23.73 of August 31ˢᵗ the lowest point of the *follow up reaction* that began on August 5ᵗʰ (15).

On September 3ʳᵈ we recognize that *buy rally* is in the making and on that same day Microsoft became a buy (15). Although Microsoft has not yet actually changed trends, the *early buy point* is the first day of the *buy rally*. See Chapter 5 Figures C.7, C8.

The *buy point* of September 3ʳᵈ is in fact a very early buy point, and looking at Figure 9.5 above we can see that Microsoft continued to rise to its high point of $29.46 on January 27, 2011. You can see that Microsoft's rise from the *early buy point* of $24.20 on September 3ʳᵈ to $29.46 on January 27ᵗʰ, 2011 is roughly 18%. We can also see it was a rather rough ascent with two large downward movements. These larger upward and downward movements large as they were did not cross over from ordinary rallies and reactions to trends.

On September 10ᵗʰ a *one day reaction* occurs because the high that day is lower than the low on the day of the *buy rally* (16) (15).

On September 14ᵗʰ an upward trend begins because the low that day is higher than the high of the *buy rally* (17) (15).

Upward trend reaches its high of $25.53 on September 17th (18).

On September 22nd a *first reaction* begins because the high that day was lower than the low of September 17th, the day the upward trend reached its high (19) (18).

On October 4th the *first reaction* reaches its low of $23.78 (20). High that day was $23.99.

A *follow up rally* begins because low this day is higher than the high of October 4th, the lowest point of the *first reaction* (21).

On October 18th the *follow up rally* high is higher than the upward trend high making a new high for the upward trend that began at (22) (18).

On October 19th a *first reaction* begins because the high that day was low than the low of on October 18th, the day the upward trend reaches its new high (23) (22).

On October 27th the *follow up rally* begins because the low that day was higher than the high on October 9th (24) (23).

The upward trend reaches its high of $27.49 on November 3rd (25).

On November 3rd a *first reaction* begins because the high that day was lower than the low on the day the upward trend reaches its high (26) (25).

On November 29th the *first reaction* reaches a low of $24.93 (27).

On December 1st a ***follow up rally*** began because the low that day was higher than the high on the day the ***first reaction*** reaches its low (28) (27).

Upward trend continues until it reaches its high of $28.40 on December 22, 2010 (29).

On December 31st a one day ***first reaction*** occurs because the high that day is lower than the low on the day the upward trend reaches its high **(30)** (29).

Upward trend reaches a new high because high that day is higher than upward trend high on December 22, 2010 **(31)** (29)

Upward trend reaches another new high **(32)**.(31).

On January 31, 2011, a one day ***first reaction*** began because the high that day was lower than the low on the day the upward trend reaches its highest point **(33)** (32).

On February 8th, a one day ***follow up rally*** occurs because that is the first day that the low of the day is higher than the high on the day the ***first reaction*** reaches its lower point **(34)** (33).

On February 10th, a ***sell reaction*** begins because the high that day was lower than the low on the day of the ***one day rally*** **(35)** (34). On this same day the low of the day is lower than the low of the ***first reaction*** on March 31st (33). This is a danger signal. On February 14th a downward trend began because the high that day is lower than the low of the ***first reaction*** on March 31st **(36)** (33).

CHAPTER 9

A Short Background of This Book "The Message Of The Tape"

The development of *The Message of The Tape* begins with Jesse Livermore and the *Livermore Market Key*. The *Livermore Market Key* first appeared in Jesse Livermore's book, "How to Trade in Stocks," published in late 1940 by Duell, Sloan & Pearce, New York. Jesse Livermore was the greatest stock operator who ever lived. At the end of his book, Livermore gave step by step instructions of his *Livermore Market Key* along with illustrative spread sheets. *The Livermore Market Key* was the method he developed over many years of stock and commodity speculation on which he relied to reveal and interpret the repetitive patterns of stock price movements. Those patterns, that is, rallies, reactions, trends and pivotal points compose *The Message of The Tape*. Those patterns, revealed by his *Livermore Market Key* method enabled Livermore to *form an opinion regarding the future trend of that stock*.

Although Livermore was very famous and demand for his book and his *Livermore Market Key* was high, the book itself and the *Livermore Market Key* were not well received by the public.

It's anybody's guess why the book was not well received. Livermore did not like charts and preferred working with actual prices in his spreadsheet format so the presentation of the *Livermore Market Key* was very difficult to work through and understand.

One look at the *Livermore Market Key* instructions and it is easy to see why few people were able to work through learning it properly, so his relatively simple method was difficult to grasp. This is indeed unfortunate because the actual *Livermore Market Key* is a relatively simple method and once grasped is very easy to work with.

But even Livermore himself stated in this book that the **Livermore Market Key** was not a "one size fits all" method for all stocks at all prices. His method applied to stocks selling at around $30.00 and he states that adjustments must be made for "very low priced issues." Unfortunately, Livermore doesn't say exactly what those adjustments are.

Within a few weeks after his book was published, Jesse Livermore committed suicide. So, whatever those adjustments were, we may never know. This also raises the question: were adjustments also required for higher priced issues?

Livermore makes other statements regarding the *Livermore Market Key* and adapting it to a "narrower market" back in 1939-40. Another unanswered question.

he basis of the *Livermore Market Key* consists of 3 and 6 point movements in stock prices. What Livermore says is that a stock selling for around $30.00 had to have a movement of at least $6.00 before he knew a rally or reaction was in the making.

After the rally or reaction ran its course and had moved in the opposite direction, or if it came back through the extreme price made on the rally or reaction by $3.00, it was either reversing or continuing its *trend*. This is illustrated below in Diagrams 1 and 2.

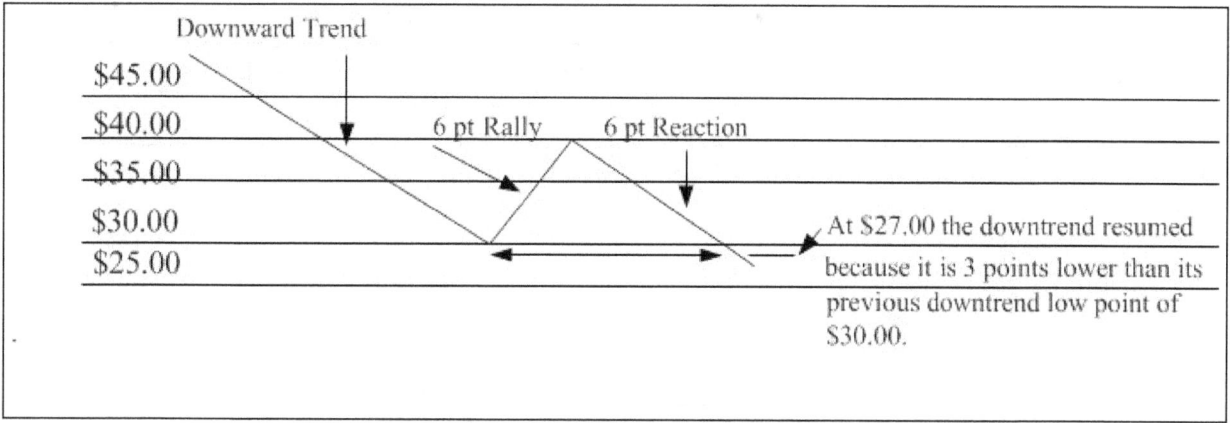

Diagram 1   Downward Trend Continues

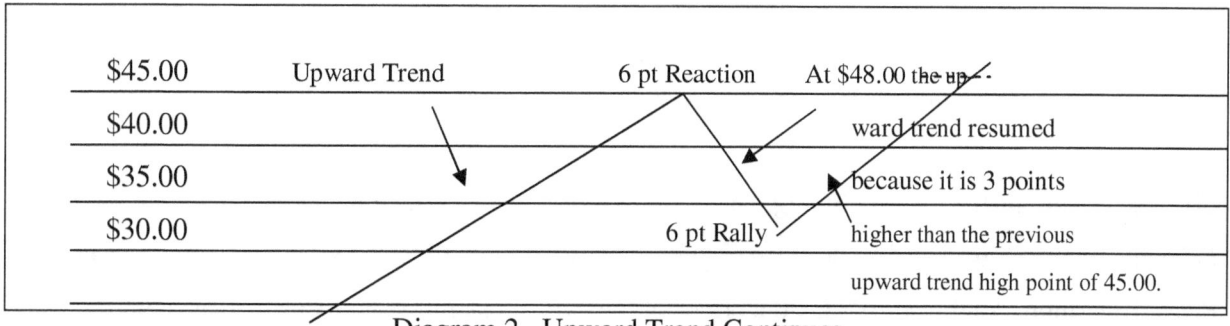

Diagram 2   Upward Trend Continues

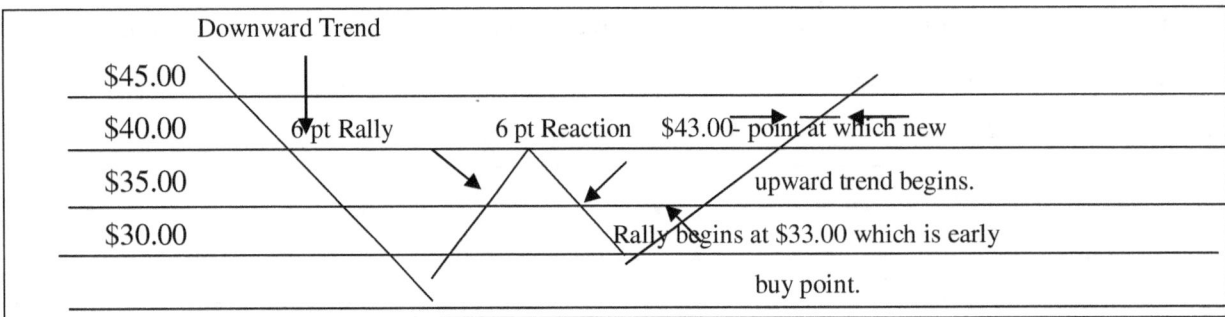

Diagram 3   Downward Trend Reverses, Begins Upward Trend

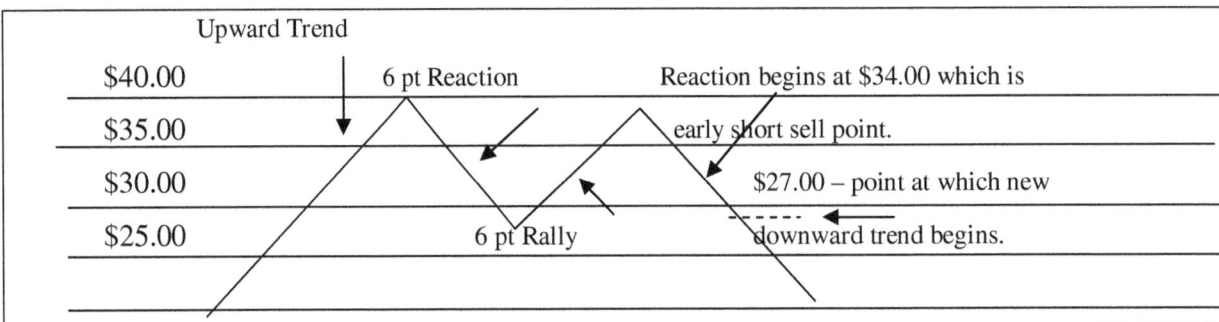

Diagram 4   Upward Trend Reverses, Becomes Downward Trend

Livermore went further by combining the action of two stocks to create his "**Key Price**". In the **Key Price** the movements were $12.00 and $6.00 instead of $3.00 and $6.00. When utilizing the **Key Price,** Livermore continued to track the prices of the two stocks individually as well as their combined total so that any change in **trend** had to be confirmed by the action of the **Key Price**. In other words, **the Key Price had to change trend in addition to** one or both of the individual stocks before he recognized the change in trend.

By doing a little arithmetic, what Livermore was saying about an individual stock selling for around $30.00 was that it needed to move 20% ($6.00) before he knew if a rally or reaction was in the making. This also means it needed to pierce that rally, reaction or trend by 10% ($3.00) to send it into a new trend or resume its present trend.

So let's assume for a moment that the "adjustment" Livermore might have been referring to for "very low priced issues" was actually the same 10% and 20% movement applying to all stocks at any price. What happens when 10% and 20% are used?

After much experimentation I have concluded that 10% and 20%, although they sound good, simply do not work. Why? Because on smaller stocks 10% and 20% produce spreads that are too narrow. On higher priced stocks it produces spreads that are too wide. Without knowing what Livermore's adjustments were and without knowing exactly how he arrived at the original 3 and 6 point movements, we are on our own to find out what it could have been *or we must find an entirely new unit of measurement.*

So, I set out to find an entirely new unit of measurement and a modified, streamlined application of that new unit of measurement for today's "narrow" and fast moving market. The new unit of measurement needed to allow *each individual stock to tell us what its own unique unit of measurement should be.* In other words, what was needed was a unit of measurement that is simple, easy to spot, requires few or no complex mathematical calculations, allows the individual stock to tell us what its own unique unit of measurement is and it must be applicable to all stocks at any price. *Not an easy measurement to find*.

I felt sure that when such a unit of measurement was discovered, if it existed at all, it would be more applicable in today's narrow, fast moving market and might also lead to the discovery of entirely new methods for revealing and expressing *The Message Of The Tape*.

After much trial and error and utilizing rules *similar* to that of the *Livermore Market Key*, I finally discovered the unit of measurement I had been looking for. This universal unit of measurement was in front of me all along but I failed to recognize it for some time.

That universal and eternal unit of measurement is the daily high and low price action of a stock as set forth in Chapter One and figures A and B.

For more on Jesse Livermore and the Livermore Market Key the following books are highly recommended:

- Reminiscences of a Stock Operator by Edwin Lefevre.
- How to Trade in Stocks by Jesse Livermore, featuring the *Livermore Market Key.*
- Jesse Livermore Worlds Greatest Stock Operator by Richard Smitten.

CHAPTER 10

Epilogue

As can be seen by Figures A and B in Chapter One, the daily fluctuation of the high and low produces the unit of measurement that results in a reliable, consistent and accurate method of measurement that identifies rallies, reaction and trends. Rallies, reactions and trends produce pivotal points. The action around pivotal points gives us the information we need to form an opinion about the present status of a stock and about possible upcoming trends.

We as learned that by using the methods in this book, it is very easy to identify rallies, reactions, pivotal points and trends. These can guide you in buying, selling and loss avoidance.

This system of measurement applies to all stocks at any price and will never change because it allows the daily high and low price of an individual stock itself to tell us where its own rallies, reactions and trends begin and end.

CHAPTER 11

Spreadsheet Version: Single Stock

Creating the Single Stock Spreadsheet

A.   Create a blank spreadsheet on 8 ½ x 11 in any spreadsheet program or any work processing program (see Fig. 1).

B.   Daily, weekly or monthly prices can be imported from Yahoo finance in a spreadsheet format (see Fig. 2).

In both A & B above, from left to right, beginning with the left most column, create the following headings:

Date, high, low natural rally, uptrend, downtrend and natural reaction (see Fig. 1).

The columns and rows need to be wide enough and high enough to allow handwritten entries. In the case of Figure 1, a column width of 10 and row height of 25 is used. Larger width for upward and downward or abbreviate and larger priced issues. Above these headings create 8-10 rows of the same width but with a smaller height of approximately 12.75 or just large enough to enter handwritten entries. Set the spreadsheet to repeat these 8-10 rows and heading rows at the top of each page. Create as many pages as necessary depending upon how far back the start date is from today.

Figure 2 – when importing from Yahoo Finance, eliminate open, close, volume and adjusted close columns. Rearrange dates from oldest to newest. Create rows, columns and column headings as in Figure 1.

Fig 1--Creating a blank spreadsheet						
			Upward Trend and Downward Trend abbreviated to save space.			
Date	High	Low	Rally	UpTrend	DnTrend	Reaction

9 Rows including colum heading row repeated at top of each page

Body of spreadsheet can have as many rows as required depending on how far back the desired start point is or how long the stock will be tracked. All data entries on this sheet are manual.

This sheet created from Yahoo Finance import to spreadsheet. Thank you Yahoo

9 Rows including colum heading row repeated at top of each page

Delete the following colums from Yahoo Finance import: open, close, volume, adjusted close

Date	High	Low	Rally	UpTrend	DnTrend	Reaction
1/3/2011	28.18	27.92				
1/4/2011	28.17	27.85				
1/5/2011	28.01	27.77				
1/6/2011	28.85	27.86				
1/7/2011	28.74	28.25				
1/10/2011	28.4	28.04				
1/11/2011	28.25	28.05				
1/12/2011	28.59	28.07				
1/13/2011	28.39	28.01				
1/14/2011	28.38	27.91				
1/18/2011	28.74	28.14				
1/19/2011	28.68	28.27				
1/20/2011	28.55	28.13				
1/21/2011	28.43	28.02				
1/24/2011	28.56	27.99				
1/25/2011	28.45	28.12				
1/26/2011	28.99	28.5				
1/27/2011	29.46	28.49				
1/28/2011	28.93	27.45				
1/31/2011	27.9	27.42				
2/1/2011	28.06	27.61				
2/2/2011	28.11	27.88				
2/3/2011	27.97	27.54				
2/4/2011	27.84	27.51				
2/7/2011	28.34	27.79				
2/8/2011	28.34	28.05				

Same row width & height as Fig 1

Single stock Spreadsheet Instructions

The last **_underlined_** price recorded in each column becomes a **_Pivotal Point_** as soon as prices are recorded in the reverse column. After a rally, reaction or trend has ended and prices are being recorded in the reverse column, the extreme price which is now underlined in the previous column becomes another **_Pivotal Point_**. It is after two **_Pivotal Points_** have been reached, and later, after several Pivotal Points have been reached that these pivotal points become of great value in anticipating correctly the next movement of importance. These Pivotal Points draw attention by having a double line drawn underneath them in either red or green. Those lines are drawn for the express purpose of keeping those Pivotal Points visible. Prices should be watched very closely whenever they are recorded at or near one of them. Your decision to act will then depend on how prices are recorded from then on.

1.) After creating the spreadsheet (from the instructions) and data is either imported from Yahoo (or any other financial) or entered manually, decide if you want to begin with the most recent 52 week high (figure 1) or most recent 52 week low (figure5). Enter the 52 week high or low the very first entry.

2.) Record prices in Upward Trend column in green. Underline in red.

3.) Record prices in Downward Trend column in red. Underline in green.

4.) Record prices in the other two columns in pencil. Underline Rally in green, Reaction in red.

5.)   _If 52 week high is desired_,

Enter the 52 week high in the Upward trend column in green and **continue to record in the Upward Trend column every day thereafter that the high price is higher than the last recorded price in the Upward Trend column** and follow instructions (**a**) through (**i**) below (**see Fig. 1**).

6.)   _If 52 week low is desired_,

Enter the 52 week low in the Downward trend column in red and **Continue to record in the Downward Trend column every day thereafter that the low price is lower than the last recorded price in the Downward Trend** and begin with (**c**) below. Then follow instructions (**a**) through (**i**) below (**see Fig. 5**).

(a) Draw red lines under the last recorded price in the Upward Trend column the first day you start to record figures in the Natural Reaction column. You begin to do this on the first day that the high price is lower than the low price on the day of the last price recorded in the Upward Trend column. Record the low price that day in the Reaction column (**see Fig. 1**). **Continue to record prices in the Natural Reaction column each day thereafter as long as the low price of the day is lower than the last recorded price in the Natural reaction column (see Fig. 1).**

(b) Draw red lines under your last recorded price in the Natural Reaction column the first day you start to record figures in the Natural Rally column. You begin to do this on the first day that the low price is higher than the high price on the day of the last recorded price in the Natural Reaction column. Record the high price that day in the Natural Rally column (**see Fig. 1**).

You now have two **_underlined_** Pivotal Points to watch: the last underlined price in the Upward Trend column and the last underlined price in the Natural Reaction column (**see Fig. 1**). Depending on how prices are recorded when the market

1

returns to near one of these points, you will then be able to form an opinion as to whether the Upward Trend is going to be resumed in earnest—or whether it has ended.

Continue to record prices in the Natural Rally column each day thereafter as long as the high price of the day is higher than the last recorded price in the Natural Rally column (see Fig. 1).

(**c**) Draw green lines under the last recorded price in the Downward Trend column the first day you start to record figures in the Natural Rally column. You begin to do this on the first day that the low price is higher than the high price on the day of the last price recorded in the Downward Trend column. Record the high price that day in the Natural Rally column (**see Fig. 5**). **Continue to record prices in the Natural Rally column each day thereafter as long as the high price of the day is higher than the last recorded price in the Natural Rally column (see Fig. 5).**

(**d**) Draw green lines under the last recorded price in the Natural Rally column the first day you begin recording in the Natural Reaction column or Downward Trend column. Record the low price of the day in the Natural reaction column or Downward Trend column on the first day that the high price of the day is lower than the low price on the day of the last recorded price in the Natural rally column. **Continue to record prices in the Natural Reaction column each day thereafter as long as the low price of the day is lower than the last recorded price in the Natural reaction column (see Fig. 5).**

You now have two *underlined* Pivotal Points to watch: the last underlined price in the Downward Trend column and the last underlined price in the Natural Rally column (**see Fig. 5**). Depending on how prices are recorded when the price returns to near one of these points, you will then be able to form an opinion as to whether the Downward Trend is going to be resumed in earnest—or whether it has ended.

(**e**) Whenever you are recording in the Natural Rally column and a high price is reached that is higher than the last price recorded in the Upward Trend column, cease recording in the Natural Rally column and record that price in green in the Upward Trend column. **Continue to record in the Upward Trend column every day thereafter that the high price is higher than the last recorded price in the Upward Trend column (see Fig. 1).**

(**f**) When recording in the Natural Rally column and a low price is reached that is higher than the last *underlined* price in the Natural Rally column, record the high price that day in green in the Upward Trend column (**see Fig. 2**). **Continue to record in the Upward Trend column every day thereafter that the high price is higher than the last recorded price in the Upward Trend.**

(**g**) When recording in the Natural Reaction column and a high price is reached that is lower than the last *underlined* price in the Natural Reaction column, the low price of that day is entered in red in the Downward Trend column (**see Fig. 2**). **Continue to record in the Downward Trend column every day thereafter that the low price is lower than the last recorded price in the Downward Trend**

2

(h) When recording figures in the Natural Reaction column and a low price is reached that is lower than the last price recorded in the Downward Trend column, cease recording in the Natural Reaction column and record that price in red in the Downward Trend column. **Continue to record in the Downward Trend column every day thereafter that the stock sells at a price which is lower than the last recorded price in the Downward Trend column (see Figs. 3 & 4).**

(i) Carry forward the last price recorded on each sheet to the upper columns on the next sheet. Also do this for each of the underlined Pivotal Point prices from each column to the same column on the next sheet. The purpose of this is to keep the Pivotal Points before you at all times **(see Figs. 2, 3, 4)**.

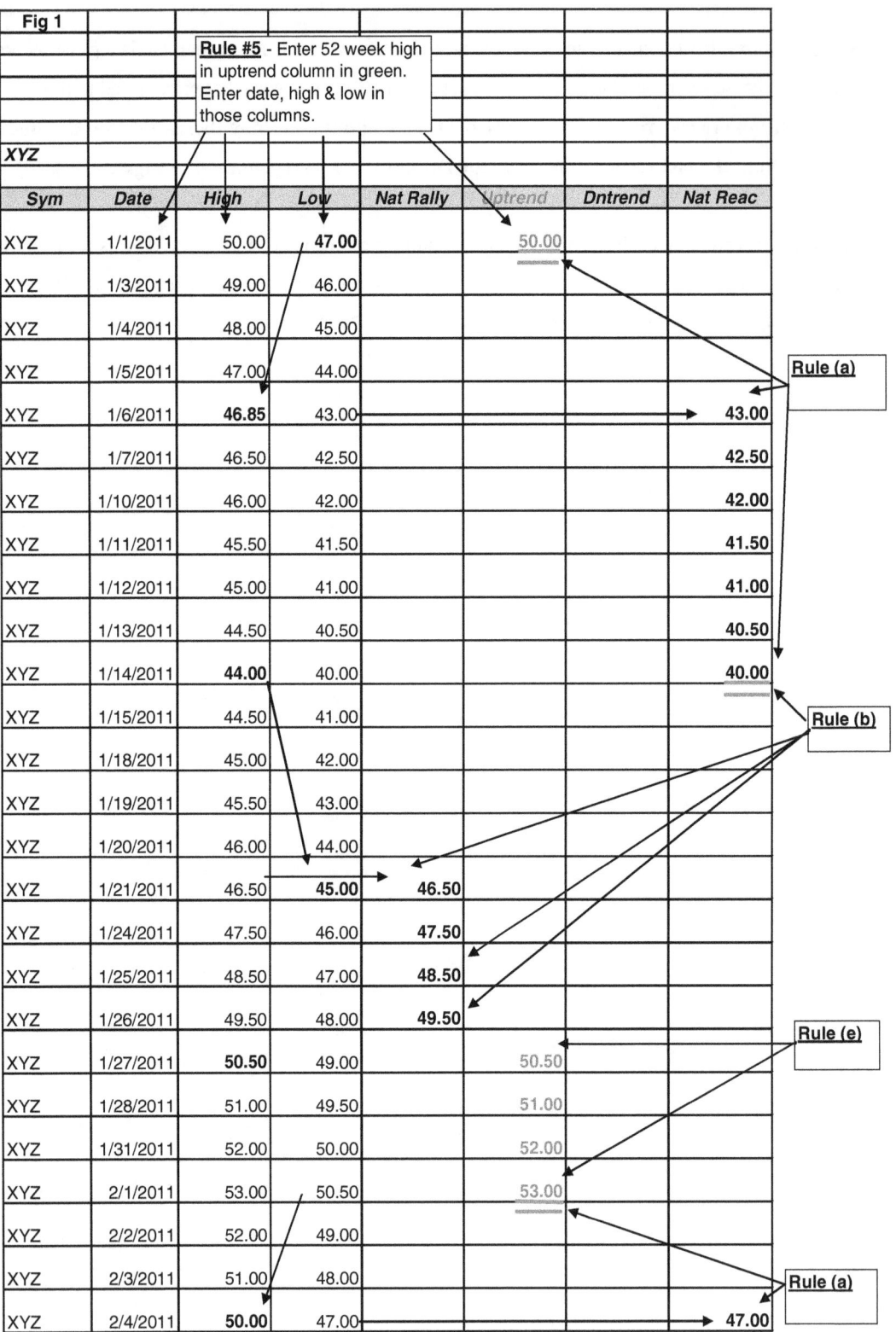

Fig 1							

Rule #5 - Enter 52 week high in uptrend column in green. Enter date, high & low in those columns.

XYZ

Sym	Date	High	Low	Nat Rally	Uptrend	Dntrend	Nat Reac
XYZ	1/1/2011	50.00	**47.00**		50.00		
XYZ	1/3/2011	49.00	46.00				
XYZ	1/4/2011	48.00	45.00				
XYZ	1/5/2011	47.00	44.00				
XYZ	1/6/2011	**46.85**	43.00				43.00
XYZ	1/7/2011	46.50	42.50				42.50
XYZ	1/10/2011	46.00	42.00				42.00
XYZ	1/11/2011	45.50	41.50				41.50
XYZ	1/12/2011	45.00	41.00				41.00
XYZ	1/13/2011	44.50	40.50				40.50
XYZ	1/14/2011	**44.00**	40.00				40.00
XYZ	1/15/2011	44.50	41.00				
XYZ	1/18/2011	45.00	42.00				
XYZ	1/19/2011	45.50	43.00				
XYZ	1/20/2011	46.00	44.00				
XYZ	1/21/2011	46.50	**45.00**	46.50			
XYZ	1/24/2011	47.50	46.00	47.50			
XYZ	1/25/2011	48.50	47.00	48.50			
XYZ	1/26/2011	49.50	48.00	49.50			
XYZ	1/27/2011	**50.50**	49.00		50.50		
XYZ	1/28/2011	51.00	49.50		51.00		
XYZ	1/31/2011	52.00	50.00		52.00		
XYZ	2/1/2011	53.00	50.50		53.00		
XYZ	2/2/2011	52.00	49.00				
XYZ	2/3/2011	51.00	48.00				
XYZ	2/4/2011	**50.00**	47.00				47.00

Rule (a)

Rule (b)

Rule (e)

Rule (a)

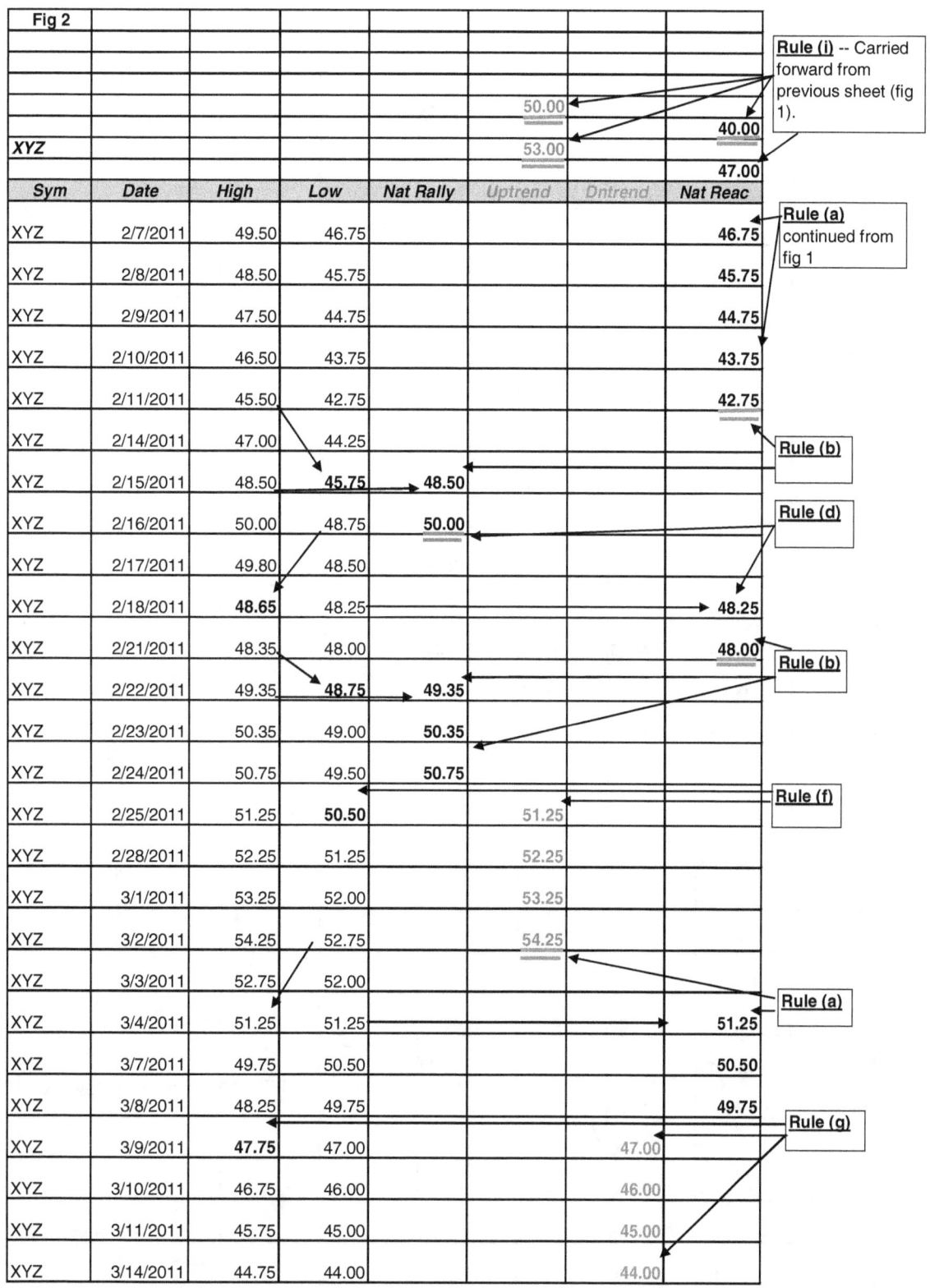

	Fig 2							
							50.00	
								40.00
	XYZ					53.00		
								47.00
Sym	Date	High	Low	Nat Rally	Uptrend	Dntrend	Nat Reac	
XYZ	2/7/2011	49.50	46.75				46.75	
XYZ	2/8/2011	48.50	45.75				45.75	
XYZ	2/9/2011	47.50	44.75				44.75	
XYZ	2/10/2011	46.50	43.75				43.75	
XYZ	2/11/2011	45.50	42.75				42.75	
XYZ	2/14/2011	47.00	44.25					
XYZ	2/15/2011	48.50	45.75	48.50				
XYZ	2/16/2011	50.00	48.75	50.00				
XYZ	2/17/2011	49.80	48.50					
XYZ	2/18/2011	48.65	48.25				48.25	
XYZ	2/21/2011	48.35	48.00				48.00	
XYZ	2/22/2011	49.35	48.75	49.35				
XYZ	2/23/2011	50.35	49.00	50.35				
XYZ	2/24/2011	50.75	49.50	50.75				
XYZ	2/25/2011	51.25	50.50		51.25			
XYZ	2/28/2011	52.25	51.25		52.25			
XYZ	3/1/2011	53.25	52.00		53.25			
XYZ	3/2/2011	54.25	52.75		54.25			
XYZ	3/3/2011	52.75	52.00					
XYZ	3/4/2011	51.25	51.25				51.25	
XYZ	3/7/2011	49.75	50.50				50.50	
XYZ	3/8/2011	48.25	49.75				49.75	
XYZ	3/9/2011	47.75	47.00			47.00		
XYZ	3/10/2011	46.75	46.00			46.00		
XYZ	3/11/2011	45.75	45.00			45.00		
XYZ	3/14/2011	44.75	44.00			44.00		

Rule (i) -- Carried forward from previous sheet (fig 1).

Rule (a) continued from fig 1

Rule (b)

Rule (d)

Rule (b)

Rule (f)

Rule (a)

Rule (g)

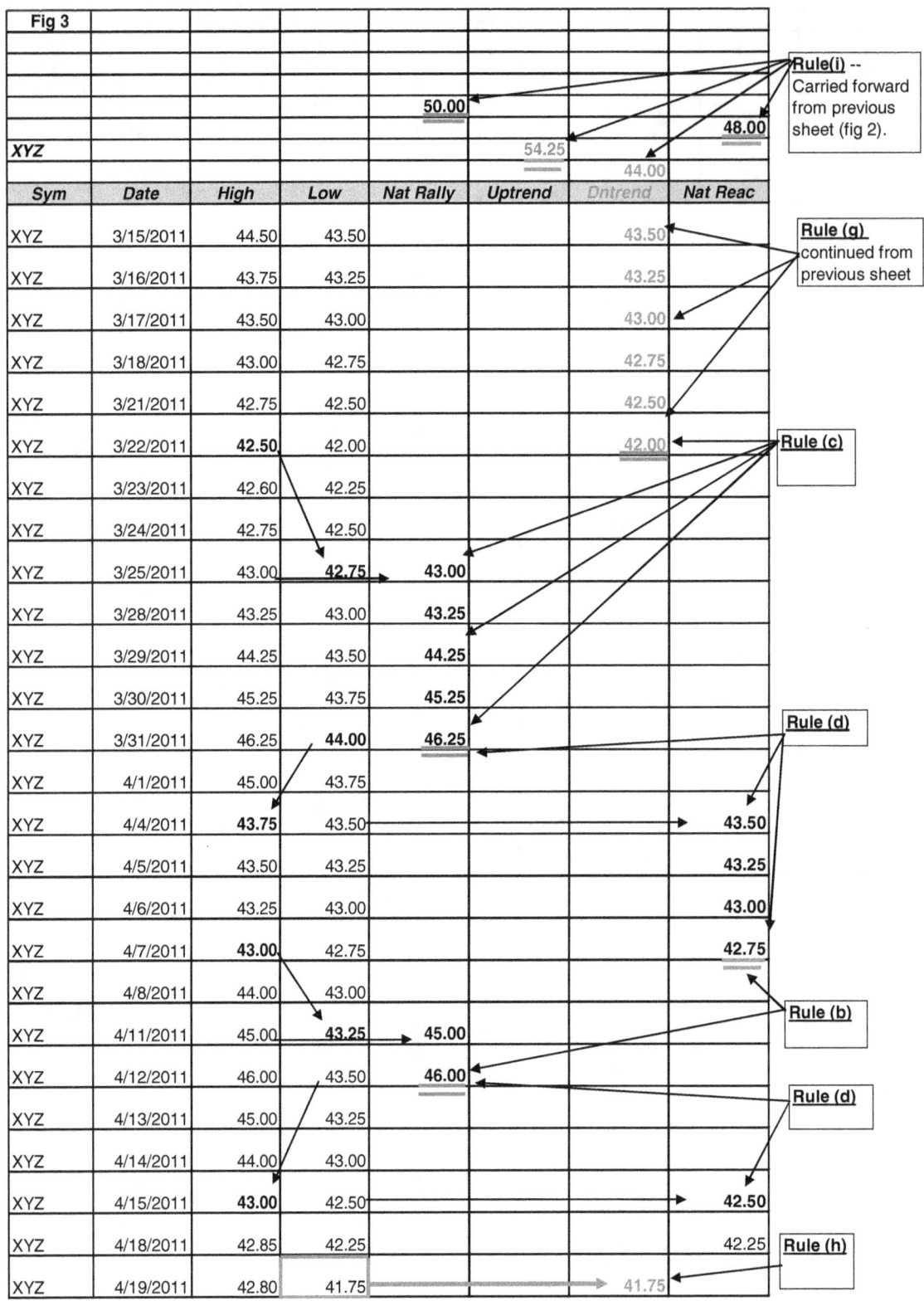

Fig 3

Rule(i) -- Carried forward from previous sheet (fig 2).

Rule (g) continued from previous sheet

Rule (c)

Rule (d)

Rule (b)

Rule (d)

Rule (h)

					50.00		48.00
XYZ					54.25	44.00	
Sym	Date	High	Low	Nat Rally	Uptrend	Dntrend	Nat Reac
XYZ	3/15/2011	44.50	43.50				43.50
XYZ	3/16/2011	43.75	43.25				43.25
XYZ	3/17/2011	43.50	43.00				43.00
XYZ	3/18/2011	43.00	42.75				42.75
XYZ	3/21/2011	42.75	42.50				42.50
XYZ	3/22/2011	42.50	42.00				42.00
XYZ	3/23/2011	42.60	42.25				
XYZ	3/24/2011	42.75	42.50				
XYZ	3/25/2011	43.00	42.75	43.00			
XYZ	3/28/2011	43.25	43.00	43.25			
XYZ	3/29/2011	44.25	43.50	44.25			
XYZ	3/30/2011	45.25	43.75	45.25			
XYZ	3/31/2011	46.25	44.00	46.25			
XYZ	4/1/2011	45.00	43.75				
XYZ	4/4/2011	43.75	43.50				43.50
XYZ	4/5/2011	43.50	43.25				43.25
XYZ	4/6/2011	43.25	43.00				43.00
XYZ	4/7/2011	43.00	42.75				42.75
XYZ	4/8/2011	44.00	43.00				
XYZ	4/11/2011	45.00	43.25	45.00			
XYZ	4/12/2011	46.00	43.50	46.00			
XYZ	4/13/2011	45.00	43.25				
XYZ	4/14/2011	44.00	43.00				
XYZ	4/15/2011	43.00	42.50				42.50
XYZ	4/18/2011	42.85	42.25				42.25
XYZ	4/19/2011	42.80	41.75			41.75	

Fig 4							
						54.25	
						42.00	
			46.25				
XYZ			46.00				42.75
						41.75	

Rule (i) -- Carried forward from previous sheet (fig 3).

Sym	Date	High	Low	Nat Rally	Uptrend	Dntrend	Nat Reac
XYZ	4/20/2011	42.00	41.50			41.50	
XYZ	4/21/2011	41.00	40.50			40.50	
XYZ	4/22/2011	40.00	39.50			39.50	
XYZ	4/25/2011	39.00	38.50			38.50	
XYZ	4/26/2011	38.00	37.50			37.50	
XYZ	4/27/2011	37.00	36.50			36.50	
XYZ	4/28/2011	36.00	35.50			35.50	
XYZ	4/29/2011	35.00	34.50			34.50	
XYZ	5/2/2011						
XYZ	5/3/2011						
XYZ	5/4/2011						
XYZ	5/5/2011						
XYZ	5/6/2011						
XYZ	5/9/2011						
XYZ	5/10/2011						
XYZ	5/11/2011						
XYZ	5/12/2011						
XYZ	5/13/2011						
XYZ	5/16/2011						
XYZ	5/17/2011						
XYZ	5/18/2011						
XYZ	5/19/2011						
XYZ	5/20/2011						
XYZ	5/23/2011						
XYZ	5/24/2011						
XYZ	5/25/2011						

Rule (h) continued from fig 3

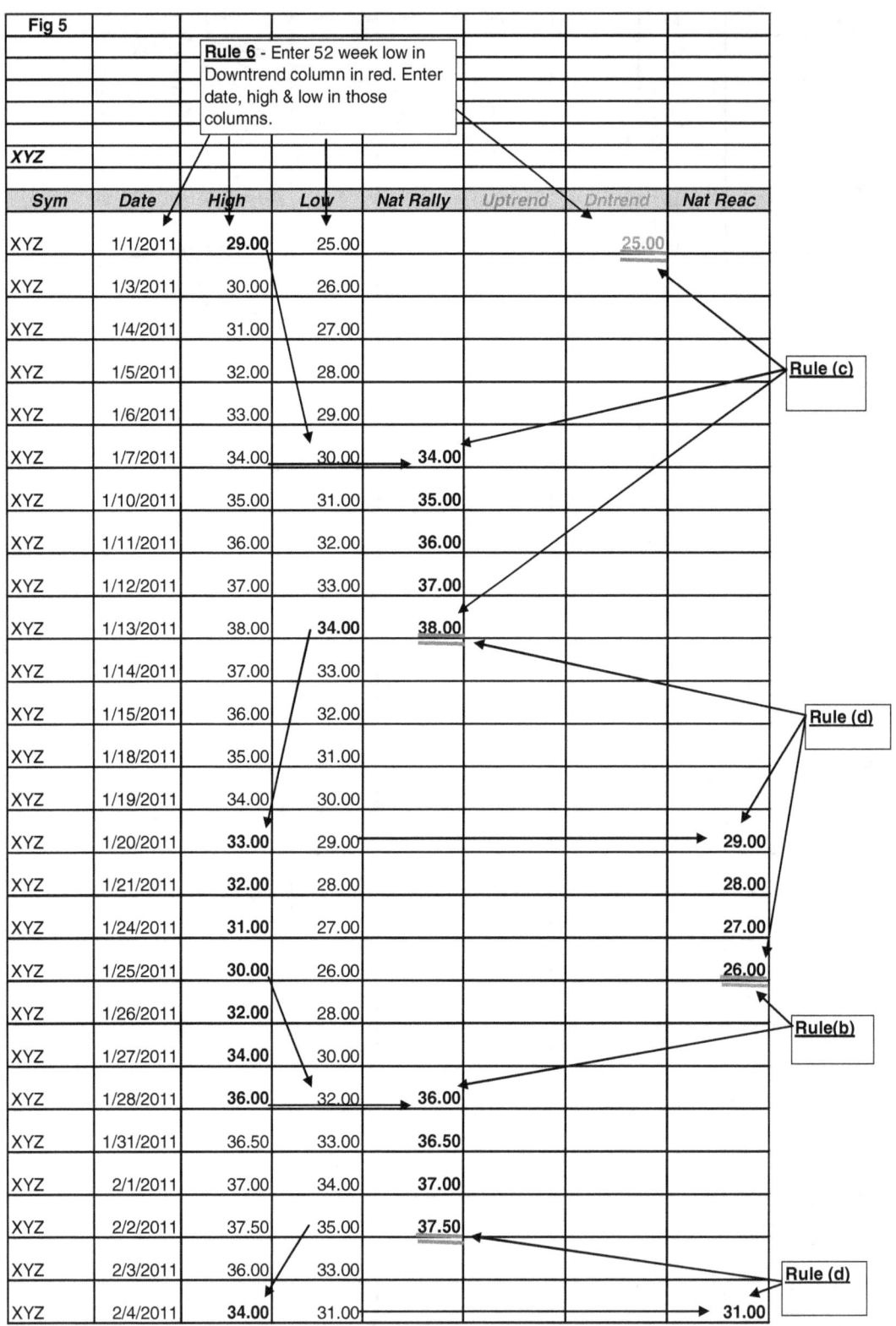

Fig 5

Rule 6 - Enter 52 week low in Downtrend column in red. Enter date, high & low in those columns.

XYZ

Sym	Date	High	Low	Nat Rally	Uptrend	Dntrend	Nat Reac
XYZ	1/1/2011	**29.00**	25.00			25.00	
XYZ	1/3/2011	30.00	26.00				
XYZ	1/4/2011	31.00	27.00				
XYZ	1/5/2011	32.00	28.00				
XYZ	1/6/2011	33.00	29.00				
XYZ	1/7/2011	34.00	30.00	**34.00**			
XYZ	1/10/2011	35.00	31.00	**35.00**			
XYZ	1/11/2011	36.00	32.00	**36.00**			
XYZ	1/12/2011	37.00	33.00	**37.00**			
XYZ	1/13/2011	38.00	**34.00**	38.00			
XYZ	1/14/2011	37.00	33.00				
XYZ	1/15/2011	36.00	32.00				
XYZ	1/18/2011	35.00	31.00				
XYZ	1/19/2011	34.00	30.00				
XYZ	1/20/2011	**33.00**	29.00				29.00
XYZ	1/21/2011	**32.00**	28.00				28.00
XYZ	1/24/2011	**31.00**	27.00				27.00
XYZ	1/25/2011	**30.00**	26.00				26.00
XYZ	1/26/2011	**32.00**	28.00				
XYZ	1/27/2011	**34.00**	30.00				
XYZ	1/28/2011	**36.00**	32.00	**36.00**			
XYZ	1/31/2011	36.50	33.00	**36.50**			
XYZ	2/1/2011	37.00	34.00	**37.00**			
XYZ	2/2/2011	37.50	35.00	**37.50**			
XYZ	2/3/2011	36.00	33.00				
XYZ	2/4/2011	**34.00**	31.00				31.00

Rule (c)

Rule (d)

Rule(b)

Rule (d)

5

CHAPTER 12

Creating the Key Price Spreadsheet

A.   Create a blank spreadsheet on 8 ½ x 14 (landscape) in any spreadsheet program or any work processing program **(see Fig. 1).**

B.   Daily, weekly or monthly prices can be imported from Yahoo finance in a spreadsheet format **(see Fig. 2).**

In both A & B above, from left to right, beginning with the left most column, create the following headings for each stock and the Key Price:

Date, high, low natural rally, uptrend, downtrend and natural reaction **(see Fig. 1)**. Abbreviate as shown.

The columns and rows need to be wide enough and high enough to allow handwritten entries. In the case of Figure 1, a column width of 10 and row height of 25 is used. Larger width for upward and downward or abbreviate and larger priced issues. Above these headings create 8-10 rows of the same width but with a smaller height of approximately 12.75 or just large enough to enter handwritten entries. Set the spreadsheet to repeat these 8-10 rows and heading rows at the top of each page. Create as many pages as necessary depending upon how far back the start date is from today or how long you intend to keep the record.

Figure 2 – when importing from Yahoo Finance, *eliminate* open, close, volume and adjusted close columns. Rearrange dates from oldest to newest. Create rows, columns and column headings for each stock and the Key Price as in **Figure 1**.

Figure 2 - *Set the Key Price high and low columns to add the daily high and low of each stock*

Follow the instructions in the next section **(a)** through **(j)** *Key Price* rules.

Figure 1-- Creating a Blank Key Price Spreadsheet

8/24/11	DAILY	DAILY					DAILY	DAILY					DAILY	DAILY				
	Key	Price																
	Key	Price																
	Key	Price																
	Key	Price																
	Key	Price																
	Key	Price																
	IBM	AAPL					IBM						AAPL					
	Key	Price					Int Bus Mach						Apple Inc.					
Date	High	Low	Nat Rally	Up Trend	Dn Trend	Nat Reac	High	Low	Nat Rally	Up Trend	Dn Trend	Nat Reac	High	Low	Nat Rally	Up Trend	Dn Trend	Nat Reac

Figure 2-- Setting Up the Key Price Spreadsheet

8/24/11

Set Key Price high & low columns to add high & low of both stocks.

Date	Key Price High	Key Price Low	Nat Rally	Up Trend	Dn Trend	Nat Reac	IBM (International Business Machines Corp) High	Low	Nat Rally	Up Trend	Dn Trend	Nat Reac	AAPL (Apple Inc.) High	Low	Nat Rally	Up Trend	Dn Trend	Nat Reac
1/3/11	478.46	471.98					148.20	147.14					330.26	324.84				
1/4/11	480.72	474.79					148.22	146.64					332.50	328.15				
1/5/11	481.82	476.23					147.48	146.73					334.34	329.50				
1/6/11	484.04	479.72					148.79	146.82					335.25	332.90				
1/7/11	485.21	478.84					148.86	146.94					336.35	331.90				
1/10/11	491.29	484.40					148.06	147.23					343.23	337.17				
1/11/11	493.31	486.22					148.35	146.75					344.96	339.47				
1/12/11	493.72	489.67					149.29	147.67					344.43	342.00				
1/13/11	495.93	492.10					149.29	148.25					346.64	343.85				
1/14/11	498.48	492.91					150.00	148.47					348.48	344.44				
1/18/11	496.23	475.38					151.47	149.38					344.76	326.00				
1/19/11	504.73	489.71					156.13	152.83					348.60	336.88				
1/20/11	494.26	484.57					155.96	154.45					338.30	330.12				
1/21/11	491.66	481.59					156.78	154.96					334.88	326.63				
1/24/11	497.24	482.05					159.79	155.33					337.45	326.72				
1/25/11	505.79	493.57					164.35	159.00					341.44	334.57				
1/26/11	507.50	501.92					161.90	160.42					345.60	341.50				
1/27/11	506.87	503.69					162.18	160.86					344.69	342.83				
1/28/11	506.32	492.20					161.92	158.67					344.40	333.53				
1/31/11	502.04	492.98					162.00	158.68					340.04	334.30				
2/1/11	509.59	502.98					163.94	162.00					345.65	340.98				

3

Rules for the Key Price

The same rules for individual stocks apply when recording the Key Price.

The last price recorded in each column becomes a Pivotal Point as soon as prices are recorded in the reverse column. After a rally, reaction or trend has ended and prices   are being recorded in the reverse column, the extreme price which is now underlined in the previous column becomes another underlined Pivotal Point. It is after two Pivotal Points have been reached, and later, after several Pivotal Points have been reached that these pivotal points become of great value in anticipating correctly the next movement of importance. These Pivotal Points draw attention by having a double line drawn underneath them in either red or green. Those lines are drawn for the express purpose of keeping those Pivotal Points visible. Prices should be watched very closely whenever they are recorded at or near one of them. Your decision to act will then depend on how prices are recorded from then on.

1.   After creating the spreadsheet (from the instructions) and data is either imported from Yahoo* (*or any other financial) or entered manually, begin by looking at the high and low price each day of each stock and the Key Price.

1a) On the first day that *both* the high price and low price are *higher* than the previous day, enter that high price in the *Upward Trend* column.

1b) If *both* the high and low price are *lower* than the previous day, enter that low price in the *Downward Trend* column.

2.   Record prices in Upward Trend column in green. Underline in red.

3.   Record prices in Downward Trend column in red. Underline in green.

4.   Record prices in the other two columns in pencil.

5. *If Upward Trend*

Continue to record in the Upward Trend column every day thereafter that the high price is higher than the last recorded price in the Upward Trend column and follow instructions (a) through (i) below (see Fig. 1).

6. *If Downward Trend*

Continue to record in the Downward Trend column every day thereafter that the low price is lower than the last recorded price in the Downward Trend and begin with (c) below. Then follow instructions (a) through (i) below.

(a) Draw red lines under the last recorded price in the Upward Trend column the first day you start to record figures in the Natural Reaction column. You begin to do this on the first day that the high price is lower than the low price on the day of the last price recorded in the Upward Trend column. Record the low price that day in the Reaction column (see Fig. 1). **Continue to record prices in the Natural Reaction column each day thereafter as long as the low price of the day is lower than the last recorded price in the Natural reaction column (see Fig. 1).**

(b) Draw red lines under your last recorded price in the Natural Reaction column the first day you start to record figures in the Natural Rally column or Upward Trend column. You begin to do this on the first day that the low price is higher than the high price on the day of the last recorded price in the Natural Reaction column. Record the high price that day in the Natural Rally column (see Fig. 1).

You now have two **_underlined_** Pivotal Points to watch: the last underlined price in the Upward Trend column and the last underlined price in the Natural Reaction column (**see Fig. 1**). Depending on how prices are recorded when the market returns to near one of these points, you will then be able to form an opinion as to whether the Upward Trend is going to be resumed in earnest—or whether it has ended.

Continue to record prices in the Natural Rally column each day thereafter as long as the high price of the day is higher than the last recorded price in the Natural Rally column (see Fig. 1).

(**c**) Draw green lines under the last recorded price in the Downward Trend column the first day you start to record figures in the Natural Rally column. You begin to do this on the first day that the low price is higher than the high price on the day of the last price recorded in the Downward Trend column. Record the high price that day in the Natural Rally column. **Continue to record prices in the Natural Rally column each day thereafter as long as the high price of the day is higher than the last recorded price in the Natural Rally column.**

(**d**) Draw green lines under the last recorded price in the Natural Rally column the first day you begin recording in the Natural Reaction column or Downward Trend column. Record the low price of the day in the Natural reaction column or Downward Trend column on the first day that the high price of the day is lower than the low price on the day of the last recorded price in the Natural rally column. **Continue to record prices in the Natural Reaction column each day thereafter as long as the low price of the day is lower than the last recorded price in the Natural reaction column.**

You now have two **_underlined_** Pivotal Points to watch: the last underlined price in the Downward Trend column and the last underlined price in the Natural Rally column. Depending on how prices are recorded when the market returns to near one of these points, you will then be able to form an opinion as to whether the Downward Trend is going to be resumed in earnest—or whether it has ended.

(**e**) Whenever you are recording in the Natural Rally column and a high price is reached that is higher than the last price recorded in the Upward Trend column, cease recording in the Natural Rally column and record that price in green in the Upward Trend column. **Continue to record in the Upward Trend column every day thereafter that the high price is higher than the last recorded price in the Upward Trend column (see Fig. 1).**

(**f**) When recording in the Natural Rally column and a low price is reached that is higher than the last **_underlined_** price in the Natural Rally column, record the high price that day in green in the Upward Trend column (**see Fig. 2**). **Continue to record in the Upward Trend column every day thereafter that the high price is higher than the last recorded price in the Upward Trend.**

(**g**) When recording in the Natural Reaction column and a high price is reached that is lower than the last **_underlined_** price in the Natural Reaction column, the low price of that day is entered in red in the Downward Trend column (**see Fig. 2**). **Continue to record in the Downward Trend column every day thereafter that the low price is lower than the last recorded price in the Downward Trend.**

(**h**) When recording figures in the Natural Reaction column and a low price is reached that is lower than the last price recorded in the Downward Trend column, cease recording in the Natural Reaction column and record that price in red in the Downward Trend column. **Continue to record in the Downward Trend column every day thereafter that the stock sells at a price which is lower than the last recorded price in the Downward Trend column (see Figs. 3 & 4).**

(**i**) Carry forward the last price recorded on each sheet to the upper columns on the next sheet. Also do this for each of the underlined Pivotal Point prices from each column to the same column on the next sheet. The purpose of this is to keep the Pivotal Points before you at all times (**See Figs. 2, 3, 4, 5, 6, 7, 8**).

(**j**) You will see, at times, that one of the stocks will change columns in unison with the Key Price even though it has not had a movement large enough to change columns. Whenever the Key Price changes from any column to another the other two stocks should be recorded in the same column as the Key Price **_as long as they are moving in the same direction as the Key Price_**. If, on the first day the Key Price changes columns, one of the two stocks is not moving in the same direction that day as the Key Price, simply watch that stock and begin to record it in the same column on the first day that it moves in the same direction as the Key Price even if it does not have a movement large enough to change columns

Key Price

Figure 1

Key Price
IBM AAPL
Key Price

Date	DAILY Key Price — High	Low	Nat Rally	Up Trend	Dn Trend	Nat Reac	IBM (Int Bus Machines Corp) — High	Low	Nat Rally	Up Trend	Dn Trend	Nat Reac	AAPL (Apple Inc.) — High	Low	Nat Rally	Up Trend	Dn Trend	Nat Reac
1/3/11	478.46	471.98					148.20	147.14					330.26	324.84				
1/4/11	480.72	474.79		480.72 ← Rule 1a			148.22	146.64		148.22 ← Rule 1(a)			332.50	328.15		332.50 ← Rule 1(a)		
1/5/11	481.82	476.23		481.82			147.48	146.73					334.34	329.50		334.34		
1/6/11	484.04	479.72		484.04			148.79	146.82		148.79			335.25	332.90		335.25		
1/7/11	485.21	478.84		485.21			148.86	146.94		148.86			336.35	331.90		336.35		
1/10/11	491.29	484.40		491.29			148.06	147.23					343.23	337.17		343.23		
1/11/11	493.31	486.22		493.31			148.35	146.75					344.96	339.47		344.96		
1/12/11	493.72	489.67		493.72			149.29	147.67		149.29			344.43	342.00		344.43		
1/13/11	495.93	492.10		495.93			149.29	148.25		149.29			346.64	343.85		346.64		
1/14/11	498.48	492.91		498.48			150.00	148.47		150.00			348.48	344.44		348.48		
1/18/11	496.23	475.38					151.47	149.38		151.47			344.76	326.00				
1/19/11	504.73	489.71		504.73			156.13	152.83		156.13			348.60	336.88		348.60 ← Rule (a)		336.88
1/20/11	494.26	484.57					155.96	154.45					338.30	330.12				
1/21/11	491.66	481.59					156.78	154.96		156.78			334.88	326.63			Rule (b)	326.63
1/24/11	497.24	482.05					159.79	155.33		159.79			337.45	326.72				
1/25/11	505.79	493.57		505.79			164.35	159.00		164.35			341.44	334.57				
1/26/11	507.50	501.92		507.50			161.90	160.42					345.60	341.50	345.60 ← Rule (d)			
1/27/11	506.87	503.69					162.18	160.86					344.69	342.83				
1/28/11	506.32	492.20					161.92	158.67					344.40	333.53				
1/31/11	502.04	492.98					162.00	158.68					340.04	334.30				334.30 ← Rule (b)
2/1/11	509.59	502.98					163.94	162.00					345.65	340.98	345.65			
2/2/11	508.85	506.16		508.85			163.60	162.61					345.25	343.55				

6

Figure 2

Key Price — Key Price / IBM AAPL / Key Price

Date	Key Price High	Key Price Low	Key Price Nat Rally	Key Price Up Trend	Key Price Dn Trend	Key Price Nat Reac	IBM (Int Bus Machines Corp) High	IBM Low	IBM Nat Rally	IBM Up Trend	IBM Dn Trend	IBM Nat Reac	AAPL (Apple Inc) High	AAPL Low	AAPL Nat Rally	AAPL Up Trend	AAPL Dn Trend	AAPL Nat Reac
2/3/11	508.44	501.36		508.85 *Rule (f)*			164.20	162.81		164.35 *Rule (f)*			344.24	338.55	345.65	348.6 *Rule (f)*		334.30 / 326.63
2/4/11	510.84	506.73		510.84			164.14	163.22					346.70	343.51	346.70	353.25 *Rule (e) & (f)*		
2/7/11	518.24	511.66		518.24			164.99	164.02					353.25	347.64		353.25 *Rule (a)*		
2/8/11	521.77	516.47		521.77			166.25	164.32		166.25 *Rule (a)*			355.52	352.15		355.52		
2/9/11	524.97	518.97		524.97			165.97	164.10					359.00	354.87		359.00		
2/10/11	525.00	511.18		525.00			165.00	163.18					360.00	348.00		360.00		
2/11/11	522.81	516.85					165.01	163.31					357.80	353.54				
2/14/11	523.86	519.56					164.38	162.85					359.48	356.71				
2/15/11	523.54	520.07					163.57	162.52				162.52 *Rule (k)*	359.97	357.55				
2/16/11	528.50	523.25		528.50 *Rule (a)*			163.60	162.75					364.90	360.50		364.90 *Rule (a)*		
2/17/11	524.94	519.37					164.67	162.85					360.27	356.52				
2/18/11	524.34	513.62					164.84	164.10	164.84 *Rule (d)*				359.50	349.52				349.52
2/22/11	509.66	499.50				499.50	164.26	161.78				161.78 *Rule (k)*	345.40	337.72				337.72 *Rule (b)*
2/23/11	507.32	498.75				498.75	162.68	160.14				160.14	344.64	338.61				
2/24/11	506.42	497.40				497.40 *Rule (b)*	161.27	159.03			159.03 *Rule (g)*		345.15	338.37				
2/25/11	510.77	505.66					162.34	160.86					348.43	344.80				
2/28/11	518.04	512.36	518.04				162.99	161.24	162.99 *Rule (k)*				355.05	351.12	355.05			
3/1/11	518.87	507.56	518.87				163.15	159.88	163.15				355.72	347.68	355.72			
3/2/11	515.46	507.81					161.11	159.41					354.35	348.40				
3/3/11	523.79	517.19	523.79				164.00	161.27	164.00				359.79	355.92	359.79			
3/4/11	524.60	518.40	524.60				164.31	160.65	164.31				360.29	357.75	360.29			
3/7/11	524.65	510.16	524.65 *Rule (d)*				162.98	158.85					361.67	351.31	361.67 *Rule (d)*			

Figure 3

Key Price

Annotations (top, boxed): Key Price — Nat Rally 524.65 (Rule (l)); Up Trend 528.5; Nat Reac 497.40 (Rule (l)). IBM — Nat Rally 164.31 / 164.84 (Rule (l)); Up Trend 166.25; Dn Trend 159.03; Nat Reac 162.52 (Rule (l)). AAPL — Nat Rally 361.67; Up Trend 364.96 (Rule (l)); Nat Reac 337.72 (Rule (l)). Other rule labels: Rule (q), Rule (d), Rule (c) (Key Price); Rule (h), Rule (e), Rule (a), Rule (c), Rule (d), Rule (k) (IBM); Rule (c), Rule (d), Rule (g) & Rule (c), Rule (b) (AAPL).

Date	Key High	Key Low	Key Nat Rally	Key Up Trend	Key Dn Trend	Key Nat Reac	IBM High	IBM Low	IBM Nat Rally	IBM Up Trend	IBM Dn Trend	IBM Nat Reac	AAPL High	AAPL Low	AAPL Nat Rally	AAPL Up Trend	AAPL Dn Trend	AAPL Nat Reac
3/8/11	520.83	511.46					163.43	159.21					357.40	352.25				
3/9/11	522.48	513.88					167.72	163.28		167.72			354.76	350.60				
3/10/11	514.44	506.28					164.67	161.38					349.77	344.90				344.90
3/11/11	515.56	505.84					163.24	160.84				160.84	352.32	345.00				
3/14/11	518.46	511.40					161.98	160.09					356.48	351.31	356.48			
3/15/11	507.48	496.98				496.98	159.64	156.88			156.88		347.84	340.10				340.10
3/16/11	499.98	477.97				477.97	156.98	151.71			151.71		343.00	326.26			326.26	
3/17/11	494.11	483.36			483.36		154.50	152.70					339.61	330.66				
3/18/11	495.15	484.32					156.95	154.32					338.20	330.00				
3/21/11	499.37	492.33					159.63	157.07	159.63				339.74	335.26				
3/22/11	501.23	496.66	501.23				158.61	157.52					342.62	339.14				
3/23/11	500.30	493.48					160.08	157.53	160.08				340.22	335.95				
3/24/11	506.71	497.70	506.71				160.71	158.84	160.71				346.00	338.86				
3/25/11	514.80	507.78	514.05				162.74	160.76	162.74				352.06	347.02	352.06			
3/28/11	516.90	511.56	516.90				162.58	161.12					354.32	350.44	354.32			
3/29/11	514.05	507.21					163.09	161.15	163.09				350.96	346.06				
3/30/11	514.87	510.46					163.99	163.02	163.99				350.88	347.44				
3/31/11	513.86	509.13					164.06	163.07	164.06				349.80	346.06				346.06
4/1/11	516.01	506.34					164.42	163.04	164.42				351.59	343.30				343.30
4/4/11	509.33	501.98				501.98	164.73	163.58	164.73				344.60	338.40				338.40
4/5/11	506.95	499.62				499.62	164.70	163.62				163.62	342.25	336.00				336.00
4/6/11	508.65	500.95					164.75	163.81					343.90	337.14				

Figure 4

Key Price

Date	High	Low	Nat Rally	Up Trend	Dn Trend	Nat Reac
(key levels)			524.65 / 516.9	528.50	483.36 / 497.40	499.62
4/7/11	504.98	499.31				499.31
4/8/11	504.53	497.11				497.11
4/11/11	499.67	493.13				493.13
4/12/11	497.50	492.50				492.50
4/13/11	501.07	496.18				
4/14/11	501.36	495.22				
4/15/11	499.98	491.67				491.67
4/18/11	498.39	483.02			483.02	
4/19/11	504.36	496.15				
4/20/11	511.64	503.69	511.64			
4/21/11	523.58	513.38	523.58			
4/25/11	522.52	517.53		522.52		
4/26/11	524.19	516.75		524.19		
4/27/11	522.94	515.56				
4/28/11	521.13	515.22				
4/29/11	526.95	517.15		526.95		
5/2/11	524.01	516.99				
5/3/11	523.37	516.85				
5/4/11	524.45	516.47				
5/5/11	521.82	513.55				
5/6/11	520.15	514.45				
5/9/11	519.05	514.84				

Rules referenced (Key Price): Rule (l), Rule (h), Rule (f), Rule (a), Rule (c)

IBM — Int Bus Machines Corp

Date	High	Low	Nat Rally	Up Trend	Dn Trend	Nat Reac
(key levels)			164.73	167.72	151.71	163.62
4/7/11	164.55	163.28				163.28
4/8/11	164.38	163.16				163.16
4/11/11	164.00	163.11			163.11	
4/12/11	163.77	162.30				162.30
4/13/11	164.93	163.66				
4/14/11	165.36	163.16				
4/15/11	166.34	164.87	166.34			
4/18/11	166.16	162.86				
4/19/11	166.38	164.44		166.38		
4/20/11	165.89	162.19				
4/21/11	168.45	164.86		168.45		
4/25/11	168.77	167.23		168.77		
4/26/11	169.20	167.40		169.20		
4/27/11	170.59	168.46		170.59		
4/28/11	171.38	169.70		171.38		
4/29/11	173.00	170.48		173.00		
5/2/11	173.54	171.49		173.54		
5/3/11	173.48	171.23				
5/4/11	172.62	169.59				
5/5/11	170.87	167.50				167.50
5/6/11	170.15	168.24				
5/9/11	169.85	168.31				

Rules referenced (IBM): Rule (l), Rule (i), Rule (b), Rule (f), Rule (a)

AAPL — Apple Inc.

Date	High	Low	Nat Rally	Up Trend	Dn Trend	Nat Reac
(key levels)			364.9 / 361.77 / 358.48 / 354.32		326.26 / 344.90	337.72 / 336.00
4/7/11	340.43	336.03				
4/8/11	340.15	333.95				333.95
4/11/11	335.67	330.02				330.02
4/12/11	333.73	330.20				
4/13/11	336.14	332.52				
4/14/11	336.00	332.06				
4/15/11	333.64	326.80				326.80
4/18/11	332.23	320.16			320.16	
4/19/11	337.98	331.71				
4/20/11	345.75	341.50				345.75
4/21/11	355.13	348.52	355.13	355.13		
4/25/11	353.75	350.30				
4/26/11	354.99	349.35				
4/27/11	352.35	347.10				
4/28/11	349.75	345.52				
4/29/11	353.95	346.67				
5/2/11	350.47	345.50				
5/3/11	349.89	345.62				
5/4/11	351.83	346.88				
5/5/11	350.95	346.05				
5/6/11	350.00	346.21				
5/9/11	349.20	346.53				

Rules referenced (AAPL): Rule (i), Rule (h), Rule (c), Rule (d) con't to next sheet

9

Figure 5

Key Price

Key Price

Date	High	Low	Nat Rally	Up Trend	Dn Trend	Nat Reac
				Key Price		
5/10/11	520.59	515.88				
5/11/11	520.52	513.06				
5/12/11	519.89	510.92				
5/13/11	518.40	509.79				
5/16/11	**511.86**	500.91		526.95	483.02	500.91
5/17/11	**507.55**	497.26				497.26
5/18/11	512.24	505.46				
5/19/11	513.81	**507.99**	513.81			
5/20/11	512.10	504.40				
5/23/11	**504.67**	496.49				496.49
5/24/11	504.57	498.85				
5/25/11	506.96	500.36				
5/26/11	504.39	500.33				
5/27/11	506.10	501.31				
5/31/11	517.72	**508.82**	517.72			
6/1/11	521.71	**511.15**	521.71			
6/2/11	515.08	510.01				
6/3/11	511.22	506.14				
6/6/11	512.63	502.08				
6/7/11	**503.46**	495.51				495.51
6/8/11	499.65	493.91				493.91
6/9/11	499.63	495.51				

Annotations: Rule (i), Rule (d), Rule (a) continued, Rule (b)

IBM — Int Bus Machines Corp

Date	High	Low	Nat Rally	Up Trend	Dn Trend	Nat Reac
			164.73	173.54	151.71	162.30
5/10/11	170.90	169.22				
5/11/11	170.52	167.82				
5/12/11	172.77	168.65				
5/13/11	172.15	169.44				
5/16/11	170.64	168.31				
5/17/11	171.41	166.53				166.53
5/18/11	171.19	169.46				
5/19/11	171.40	169.32				
5/20/11	171.15	169.38				
5/23/11	168.69	167.07				
5/24/11	168.67	167.51				
5/25/11	168.40	167.51				
5/26/11	167.50	165.90				165.90
5/27/11	168.47	167.00				
5/31/11	169.89	167.82				
6/1/11	169.58	166.50				
6/2/11	167.10	165.71				165.71
6/3/11	165.89	164.13				164.13
6/6/11	165.58	164.27				
6/7/11	165.24	163.61				163.61
6/8/11	164.85	163.26				163.26
6/9/11	165.96	164.76				

Annotation: Rule (l), 167.50

AAPL — Apple Inc.

Date	High	Low	Nat Rally	Up Trend	Dn Trend	Nat Reac
			355.13 / 354.32		320.16	
5/10/11	349.69	346.66				
5/11/11	350.00	345.24				
5/12/11	**347.12**	342.27				
5/13/11	346.25	340.35				340.35
5/16/11	341.22	332.60				332.60
5/17/11	**336.14**	330.73				330.73
5/18/11	341.05	336.00				
5/19/11	342.41	**338.67**	342.41			
5/20/11	340.95	335.02				
5/23/11	**335.98**	329.42				329.42
5/24/11	335.90	331.34				
5/25/11	338.56	332.85				
5/26/11	336.89	334.43				
5/27/11	337.63	334.31				
5/31/11	347.83	**341.00**	347.83			
6/1/11	352.13	**344.65**	352.13			
6/2/11	347.98	344.30				
6/3/11	345.33	342.01				
6/6/11	347.05	337.81				
6/7/11	**338.22**	331.90				331.90
6/8/11	334.80	330.65				330.65
6/9/11	333.67	330.75				

Annotations: Rule (l), Rule (d), Rule (b), Rule (f), Rule (a)

Figure 6

Key Price — DAILY

Date	High	Low	Nat Rally	Up Trend	Dn Trend	Nat Reac
	513.81 (Rule (l))		521.71			493.91 / 496.49
6/10/11	496.50	488.38				
6/13/11	492.77	487.80			487.8 (Rule (a))	
6/14/11	497.82	492.96	497.82 (Rule (c))			
6/15/11	493.71	486.40				
6/16/11	492.31	480.11			480.11 (Rule (d))	
6/17/11	494.35	482.94				
6/20/11	483.31	474.09			474.09 (Rule (c))	488.38
6/21/11	492.55	479.20				
6/22/11	495.71	487.48	495.71			
6/23/11	498.42	481.92	498.42			
6/24/11	499.09	489.66	499.09			
6/27/11	502.14	492.46	502.14			
6/28/11	507.40	501.45	507.40	507.40 (Rule (f))		
6/29/11	507.23	501.70				
6/30/11	508.58	503.59		508.58		
7/1/11	518.15	505.69		518.15		
7/5/11	525.26	516.02		525.26		
7/6/11	531.87	521.80		531.87		
7/7/11	535.27	530.12		535.27		
7/8/11	536.49	527.21		536.49		
7/11/11	535.92	527.43				
7/12/11	533.05	522.51				

IBM — Int Bus Machines Corp — DAILY

Date	High	Low	Nat Rally	Up Trend	Dn Trend	Nat Reac
			164.73 (Rule (l))	173.54		162.30 / 163.26
			151.71			
6/10/11	164.84	162.87				
6/13/11	164.46	162.73			162.73 (Rule (k))	162.87
6/14/11	164.57	163.65				
6/15/11	163.63	161.52			161.52 (Rule (c))	
6/16/11	163.41	161.78				
6/17/11	165.10	163.58	165.10			
6/20/11	165.61	163.59	165.61			
6/21/11	166.75	164.00	166.75			
6/22/11	166.81	165.10	166.81			
6/23/11	166.73	163.80				
6/24/11	165.94	164.57				
6/27/11	168.24	165.21				
6/28/11	170.70	168.01	170.70	170.70 (Rule (k))		
6/29/11	170.86	169.82		170.86		
6/30/11	172.45	170.75		172.45		
7/1/11	174.65	171.49		174.65		
7/5/11	175.43	173.52		175.43		
7/6/11	177.77	175.09		177.77		
7/7/11	177.27	176.12				
7/8/11	176.49	175.01				
7/11/11	176.15	174.61				
7/12/11	175.37	173.89				

AAPL — Apple Inc. — DAILY

Date	High	Low	Nat Rally	Up Trend	Dn Trend	Nat Reac
			342.41 (Rule (l))	352.13	325.07	329.42 / 330.65
6/10/11	331.66	325.51				325.51
6/13/11	328.31	325.07			325.07 (Rule (c))	
6/14/11	333.25	329.31	333.25 (Rule (d))			
6/15/11	330.30	324.88				
6/16/11	328.68	318.33	329.31		318.33 (Rule (h))	
6/17/11	329.25	319.36				
6/20/11	317.70	310.50			310.50 (Rule (c))	325.51
6/21/11	325.80	315.20				
6/22/11	328.90	322.38	328.90			
6/23/11	331.69	318.12	331.69			
6/24/11	333.15	325.09	333.15			
6/27/11	333.90	327.25	333.90			
6/28/11	336.70	333.44		336.70 (Rule (f))		
6/29/11	336.37	331.88				
6/30/11	336.13	332.84				
7/1/11	343.50	334.20		343.50		
7/5/11	349.83	342.50		349.83		
7/6/11	354.10	346.71		351.10		
7/7/11	358.00	354.00		358.00		
7/8/11	360.00	352.20		360.00		
7/11/11	359.77	352.82				
7/12/11	357.68	348.62				

Figure 7

Key Price

Date	Key Price High	Key Price Low	Nat Rally	Up Trend	Dn Trend	Nat Reac	IBM High	IBM Low	Nat Rally	Up Trend	Dn Trend	Nat Reac	AAPL High	AAPL Low	Nat Rally	Up Trend	Dn Trend	Nat Reac
				Key Price					**IBM** Int Bus Machines Corp						**AAPL** Apple Inc.			
7/13/11	536.32	530.38					176.32	174.00					360.00	356.38				
7/14/11	537.71	530.18		537.71			176.10	173.84					361.61	356.34		361.61		
7/15/11	540.94	533.24		540.94			175.94	174.07					365.00	359.17		365.00		
7/18/11	551.11	538.86		551.11			176.46	173.58					374.65	365.28		374.65		
7/19/11	563.86	551.97		563.96			185.21	178.65		185.21			378.65	373.32		378.65		
7/20/11	580.69	569.00		580.69			184.42	183.00					396.27	386.00		396.27		
7/21/11	575.56	566.80					185.50	182.90		185.50			390.06	383.90				
7/22/11	580.68	572.01					185.63	**184.26**		185.63			395.05	387.75				
7/25/11	584.96	572.90		584.96			184.96	183.28					400.00	389.62		400.00		
7/26/11	588.55	**582.33**		588.55			184.05	182.65				182.65	404.50	**399.68**		404.50		
7/27/11	585.55	573.08					182.91	180.93				180.93	402.64	392.15				
7/28/11	**580.26**	569.01				569.01	183.27	180.88				180.88	**396.99**	388.13				388.13
7/29/11	578.58	563.73				563.73	183.43	179.73				179.73	395.15	384.00				384.00
8/1/11	583.19	570.87					183.69	178.50				178.50	399.50	392.37				
8/2/11	580.19	566.21					182.29	177.86				177.86	397.90	388.35				
8/3/11	572.78	557.65				557.65	179.23	175.41				175.41	393.55	382.24				382.24
8/4/11	569.24	548.53				548.53	177.92	171.18				171.18	391.32	377.35				377.35
8/5/11	557.72	529.09				529.09	174.22	166.52				166.52	383.50	362.57				362.57
8/8/11	540.38	519.02				519.02	172.61	166.00				166.00	**367.77**	353.02				353.02
8/9/11	**545.66**	517.00				517.00	171.05	162.00				162.00	374.61	355.00				
8/10/11	543.88	524.35					**169.23**	161.85				161.85	374.65	362.50				
8/11/11	544.22	527.66					168.77	162.94					375.45	364.72				

Annotations — Key Price Rule (i): Nat Rally 497.82; Up Trend 536.49; Dn Trend 487.80 / 474.09. Rule (a). Rule (b).

Annotations — IBM Rule (i): Nat Rally 164.73; Up Trend 173.54 / 177.77; Dn Trend 162.30 / 161.52. Rule (a). Rule (b).

Annotations — AAPL Rule (i): Nat Rally 333.25; Up Trend 360.00; Dn Trend 310.50. Rule (a). Rule (b).

Figure 8

Key Price

Key Price

Date	High	Low	Nat Rally	Up Trend	Dn Trend	Nat Reac
Key Price			497.82	588.55	474.09	517.00
8/12/11	549.02	540.06				
8/15/11	558.97	**548.48**	558.97			
8/16/11	555.56	545.06				
8/17/11	557.51	547.89				

Rule (l) — Rule (b) continued

IBM — Int Bus Machines Corp

High	Low	Nat Rally	Up Trend	Dn Trend	Nat Reac
			185.63	161.52	161.85
169.38	165.83				
174.00	**170.39**	174.00			
172.19	169.00				
172.99	169.89				

Rule (l) — Rule (b) continued

AAPL — Apple Inc.

High	Low	Nat Rally	Up Trend	Dn Trend	Nat Reac
		333.25	404.50	310.50	353.02
379.64	**374.23**	379.64			
384.97	378.09	384.97			
383.37	376.06				
384.52	378.00				

Rule (b) continued

13

This whole Method

This whole method is designed, when a stock is in an Upward Trend or Downward Trend, to enable one to see clearly whether a stock is acting the way it ought to, after its *first* Natural Rally or Reaction has occurred. If the movement is going to be resumed in a positive manner—either up or down—it will carry through the *Trend* Pivotal Point by the proper amount. That means if it's in an Upward Trend it will carry through the Upward Trend pivotal point to where the low of the day will be higher than the high of the Upward Trend pivotal point **(See Fig. 1)**. If it's in a Downward Trend it will carry through the Downward Trend pivotal point to where the high of the day will be lower than the low of the Downward Trend pivotal point **(See Fig. 2)**.

(a) If the stock is in an Upward Trend and it experiences its *first reaction,* we are now watching for the follow up rally. If, During the follow up rally, the high price *pierces* the Upward Trend pivotal point but does not carry through to where the low of the day is higher than the high of the Upward Trend pivotal point—and in a subsequent reaction the high of the day is lower than the low of that last *underlined* Upward Trend Pivotal Point, it would indicate that the Upward Trend in the stock is over (See Fig. 3).

(b) When recording in the Natural Rally column, if the high price of the rally ends a short distance below the low of the last underlined Pivotal Point in the Upward Trend column, and the stock reacts from the high of that rally to where the high of the day is lower than the low on the day the Rally reached its high, it is a danger signal, which would indicate the Upward Trend in that stock is over. (See Fig. 4).

(c) If the stock is in a Downward Trend and it experiences its *first rally,* we are now watching for the follow up reaction. If, during the follow up reaction, the low price *pierces* the Downward Trend pivotal point but does not carry through to where the high of the day is lower than the low of the Downward Trend pivotal point—and in a subsequent rally the low of the day is higher than the high of that last *underlined* Downward Trend Pivotal Point, it would indicate that the Downward Trend in the stock is over (See Fig. 5).

(d) When recording in the Natural Reaction column, if the low price of the reaction ends a short distance above the high of the last underlined Pivotal Point in the Downward Trend column, and the stock rallies from the low of that reaction where the low of the day is higher than the high on the day the reaction reached its low, it is a danger signal, which would indicate the Downward Trend in that stock is over. (See Fig. 6).

(e) Whenever a stock is in a Rally and experiences a reaction and that reaction is followed by a rally, we are watching carefully to see if a new trend will be formed by the action of that rally. On the first day the low of the rally is higher than the high of the previous underlined rally. That is the first day of a new Upward Trend. (See Fig. 7).

(f) Whenever a stock is in a Reaction and experiences a rally and that rally is followed by a reaction, we are watching carefully to see if a new trend will be formed by the action of that reaction. On the first day the high of the reaction is lower than the low of the previous underlined reaction. That is the first day of a new Downward Trend. (See Fig. 8).

All of this boils down to:

(a) When green lines are drawn below the last recorded red figure in the Downward Trend column—you may be given a signal to buy if the stock returns to near that point. ***See Rule (c), Fig. 5.***

(b) When green lines are drawn below the last price recorded in the Natural Rally column, and if the stock on its next rally reaches a point near that Pivotal Point price, that is when you are going to find out if the market is strong enough to pierce that Pivotal Point and change course into the Upward Trend column. ***See Rule (e), Fig. 7.***

(c) The reverse holds true when red lines are drawn under the last price recorded in the Upward Trend column —you may be given a signal to buy, sell or sell short if the stock returns to near that point. ***See Fig. 1 and Rule (a), Fig. 3.***

(d) When red lines are drawn below the last price recorded in the Natural Reaction column, and if the stock on its next reaction reaches a point near that Pivotal Point price, that is when you are going to find out if the market is strong enough to pierce that Pivotal Point and change course into the Downward Trend column. ***See Rule (f), Fig. 8.***

XYZ

Sym	Date	High	Low	Nat Rally	Uptrend	Dntrend	Nat Reac
XYZ	1/1/2011	50.00	46.00		**50.00**		
XYZ	1/2/2011	51.00	47.00		**51.00**		
XYZ	1/3/2011	52.00	48.00		**52.00**		
XYZ	1/4/2011	53.00	**49.00**		**53.00**		
XYZ	1/5/2011	52.00	48.00				
XYZ	1/6/2011	51.00	47.00				
XYZ	1/7/2011	50.00	46.00				
XYZ	1/8/2011	49.00	45.00				
XYZ	1/9/2011	**48.00**	44.00		*First Reaction*		44.00
XYZ	1/10/2011	47.00	43.00				43.00
XYZ	1/11/2011	46.00	42.00				42.00
XYZ	1/12/2011	45.00	41.00				41.00
XYZ	1/13/2011	**44.00**	40.00				40.00
XYZ	1/14/2011	46.00	42.00				
XYZ	1/15/2011	48.00	44.00		*Follow Up Rally*		
XYZ	1/16/2011	50.00	**46.00**	50.00			
XYZ	1/17/2011	52.00	**48.00**	52.00			
XYZ	1/18/2011	54.00	50.00		54.00		
XYZ	1/19/2011	56.00	52.00		56.00		
XYZ	1/20/2011	58.00	**54.00**		58.00		
XYZ	1/21/2011						
XYZ	1/22/2011						
XYZ	1/23/2011						
XYZ	1/24/2011						
XYZ	1/25/2011						
XYZ	1/26/2011						

Upward Trend will probably continue because low of 54.00 on 1/20 is higher than the last underlined Pivotal Point of 53.00 in the Uptrend column. This means price has carried through that previous Uptrend pivotal point by the proper amount *after* its *First Reaction*.

XYZ

Sym	Date	High	Low	Nat Rally	Uptrend	Dntrend	Nat Reac
XYZ	1/1/2011	44.50	43.50			43.50	
XYZ	1/2/2011	43.75	43.25			43.25	
XYZ	1/3/2011	43.50	43.00			43.00	
XYZ	1/4/2011	43.00	42.75			42.75	
XYZ	1/5/2011	42.75	42.50			42.50	
XYZ	1/6/2011	**42.50**	42.00			42.00	←
XYZ	1/7/2011	42.60	42.25				
XYZ	1/8/2011	42.75	42.50				
XYZ	1/9/2011	43.00	**42.75**	43.00	First Rally		
XYZ	1/10/2011	43.25	43.00	**43.25**			
XYZ	1/11/2011	44.25	43.50	**44.25**			
XYZ	1/12/2011	45.25	43.75	**45.25**			
XYZ	1/13/2011	46.25	**44.00**	**46.25**			
XYZ	1/14/2011	45.00	43.75				
XYZ	1/15/2011	**43.75**	43.50		Follow Up Reaction		**43.50**
XYZ	1/16/2011	43.50	43.25				**43.25**
XYZ	1/17/2011	43.25	41.75			41.75	
XYZ	1/18/2011	43.00	41.50			41.50	
XYZ	1/19/2011	44.00	41.00			41.00	
XYZ	1/20/2011	43.00	40.00			40.00	
XYZ	1/21/2011	42.00	39.00			39.00	
XYZ	1/22/2011	41.00	38.00			38.00	
XYZ	1/23/2011	40.00	37.00			37.00	
XYZ	1/24/2011	39.00	36.00			36.00	
XYZ	1/25/2011	38.00	35.00			35.00	
XYZ	1/26/2011	37.00	34.00			34.00	

Downward Trend will probably continue because high of 41.00 on 1/22 is lower than the last underlined Pivotal Point of 42.00 in the Downtrend column. This means price has carried through that previous Downtrend pivotal point by the proper amount after its First Reaction.

	Trend rule (a) fig 3						
XYZ							
Sym	Date	High	Low	Nat Rally	Uptrend	Dntrend	Nat Reac
XYZ	1/1/2011	50.00	**47.00**		50.00		
XYZ	1/3/2011	49.00	46.00				
XYZ	1/4/2011	48.00	45.00				
XYZ	1/5/2011	47.00	44.00				
XYZ	1/6/2011	**46.85**	43.00			*First Reaction*	**43.00**
XYZ	1/7/2011	46.50	42.50				**42.50**
XYZ	1/10/2011	46.00	42.00				**42.00**
XYZ	1/11/2011	45.50	41.50				**41.50**
XYZ	1/12/2011	45.00	41.00				**41.00**
XYZ	1/13/2011	44.50	40.50				**40.50**
XYZ	1/14/2011	**44.00**	40.00				**40.00**
XYZ	1/15/2011	44.50	41.00				
XYZ	1/18/2011	45.00	42.00				
XYZ	1/19/2011	45.50	43.00	*Follow Up Rally*			
XYZ	1/20/2011	46.00	44.00				
XYZ	1/21/2011	46.50	**45.00**	**46.50**			
XYZ	1/24/2011	47.50	46.00	**47.50**			
XYZ	1/25/2011	48.50	47.00	**48.50**			
XYZ	1/26/2011	49.50	48.00	**49.50**			
XYZ	1/27/2011	**50.50**	49.00		50.50		
XYZ	1/28/2011	51.00	49.50		51.00		
XYZ	1/31/2011	50.00	49.00				
XYZ	2/1/2011	**48.50**	48.00			*Sell Reaction*	**48.00**
XYZ	2/2/2011	48.00	47.00				**47.00**
XYZ	2/3/2011	47.00	46.00				**46.00**
XYZ	2/4/2011	46.00	45.00				**45.00**

Rule (a) - Follow Up Rally eventually breaks through **Upward Trend** Pivotal Point of 50.00 but low price on 1/28 is not higher than 50.00 and a **Sell Reaction** begins on 2/1. This indicates **Upward Trend** is probably over.

Fig 4 Trend rule (b)

XYZ

Sym	Date	High	Low	Nat Rally	Uptrend	Dntrend	Nat Reac
XYZ	1/1/2011	50.00	**47.00**		50.00		
XYZ	1/3/2011	49.00	46.00				
XYZ	1/4/2011	48.00	45.00				
XYZ	1/5/2011	47.00	44.00				
XYZ	1/6/2011	**46.85**	43.00				43.00
XYZ	1/7/2011	46.50	42.50				42.50
XYZ	1/10/2011	46.00	42.00				42.00
XYZ	1/11/2011	45.50	41.50				41.50
XYZ	1/12/2011	45.00	41.00				41.00
XYZ	1/13/2011	44.50	40.50				40.50
XYZ	1/14/2011	**44.00**	40.00				40.00
XYZ	1/15/2011	44.50	41.00				
XYZ	1/18/2011	45.00	42.00				
XYZ	1/19/2011	45.50	43.00				
XYZ	1/20/2011	46.00	44.00				
XYZ	1/21/2011	46.50	**45.00**	46.50			
XYZ	1/24/2011	47.50	46.00	47.50			
XYZ	1/25/2011	48.50	47.00	48.50			
XYZ	1/26/2011	49.85	49.00	**49.85**			
XYZ	1/27/2011	49.75	48.85				
XYZ	1/28/2011	49.50	48.75				
XYZ	1/31/2011	49.25	48.60				
XYZ	2/1/2011	**48.50**	48.00				48.00
XYZ	2/2/2011	48.00	47.00				47.00
XYZ	2/3/2011	47.00	46.00				46.00
XYZ	2/4/2011	46.00	45.00				45.00

First Reaction

Follow Up Rally

Sell Reaction

Rule (b)- **Follow Up Rally** ends a short distance below last **Upward Trend** Pivotal Point of 50.00 and a **Sell Reaction** begins on 2/1. This indicates **Upward Trend** is probably over.

Fig 5 Trend Rule (c)

XYZ

Sym	Date	High	Low	Nat Rally	Uptrend	Dntrend	Nat Reac
XYZ	3/15/2011	44.50	43.50			43.50	
XYZ	3/16/2011	43.75	43.25			43.25	
XYZ	3/17/2011	43.50	43.00			43.00	
XYZ	3/18/2011	43.00	42.75			42.75	
XYZ	3/21/2011	42.75	42.50			42.50	
XYZ	3/22/2011	**42.50**	42.00			42.00	
XYZ	3/23/2011	42.60	42.25				
XYZ	3/24/2011	42.75	42.50				
XYZ	3/25/2011	43.00	**42.75**	43.00	*First Rally*		
XYZ	3/28/2011	43.25	43.00	**43.25**			
XYZ	3/29/2011	44.25	43.50	**44.25**			
XYZ	3/30/2011	45.25	43.75	**45.25**			
XYZ	3/31/2011	46.25	**44.00**	**46.25**			
XYZ	4/1/2011	45.00	43.75				
XYZ	4/4/2011	**43.75**	43.50		*Follow Up Reaction*		**43.50**
XYZ	4/5/2011	43.50	43.25				**43.25**
XYZ	4/6/2011	43.25	41.75			41.75	
XYZ	4/7/2011	43.00	41.50			41.50	
XYZ	4/8/2011	44.00	41.00			41.00	
XYZ	4/11/2011	45.00	**44.25**	45.00	*Buy Rally*		
XYZ	4/12/2011	46.00	43.50	**46.00**			
XYZ	4/13/2011	46.50	43.75	**46.50**			
XYZ	4/14/2011	46.75	44.00	**46.75**			
XYZ	4/15/2011	47.00	44.25	**47.00**			
XYZ	4/18/2011	47.25	44.50	**47.25**			
XYZ	4/19/2011	47.50	44.75	**47.50**			

Rule (c)- *Follow Up Reaction* eventually breaks through *Downward Trend* Pivotal Point of 42.00 but high price on 4/8 is not lower than 42.00 and a *Buy Rally* begins on 4/11. This indicates *Downward Trend* is probably over.

Fig 6 Trend rule (d)

XYZ

Sym	Date	High	Low	Nat Rally	Uptrend	Dntrend	Nat Reac
XYZ	2/7/2011	49.50	46.75			46.75	
XYZ	2/8/2011	48.50	45.75			45.75	
XYZ	2/9/2011	47.50	44.75			44.75	
XYZ	2/10/2011	46.50	43.75			43.75	
XYZ	2/11/2011	45.50	42.75			42.75	
XYZ	2/14/2011	47.00	44.25				
XYZ	2/15/2011	48.50	**45.75**	**48.50**	*First Rally*		
XYZ	2/16/2011	50.00	48.75	**50.00**			
XYZ	2/17/2011	49.80	48.50				
XYZ	2/18/2011	**48.65**	48.25		*Follow Up Reaction*		48.25
XYZ	2/21/2011	48.35	48.00				48.00
XYZ	2/22/2011	48.00	47.00				47.00
XYZ	2/23/2011	47.75	45.00				45.00
XYZ	2/24/2011	**47.50**	44.00				44.00
XYZ	2/25/2011	47.25	43.00				43.00
XYZ	2/28/2011	48.25	44.75				
XYZ	3/1/2011	49.25	46.75				
XYZ	3/2/2011	50.25	**47.75**	**50.25**			
XYZ	3/3/2011	50.50	48.00	**50.50**			
XYZ	3/4/2011	50.75	48.25	**50.75**			
XYZ	3/7/2011	51.00	47.50	**51.00**			
XYZ	3/8/2011	51.25	46.75	**51.25**			
XYZ	3/9/2011						
XYZ	3/10/2011						
XYZ	3/11/2011						
XYZ	3/14/2011						

Rule (d)- *Follow Up Reaction* ends at 43.00, a short distance above last ***Downward Trend*** Pivotal Point of 42.75. A ***Buy Rally*** begins on 3/2. This indicates ***Downward Trend*** is probably over.

	Fig 7 Rally / Reac Trend Change (e)						

XYZ

Sym	Date	High	Low	Nat Rally	Uptrend	Dntrend	Nat Reac
XYZ	1/1/2011	**22.00**	18.00	**22.00**			
XYZ	1/2/2011	26.00	**23.00**	**26.00**			
XYZ	1/3/2011	27.00	**24.00**	27.00			
XYZ	1/4/2011	26.00	23.00				
XYZ	1/5/2011	25.00	22.00			Reaction	
XYZ	1/6/2011	24.00	21.00				
XYZ	1/7/2011	**23.00**	20.00				**20.00**
XYZ	1/8/2011	22.00	19.00				**19.00**
XYZ	1/9/2011	21.00	18.00				**18.00**
XYZ	1/10/2011	**20.00**	17.00				**17.00**
XYZ	1/11/2011	21.00	18.00	Rally			
XYZ	1/12/2011	22.00	20.50	**22.00**			
XYZ	1/13/2011	23.00	20.00	**23.00**			
XYZ	1/14/2011	24.00	**21.00**	24.00			
XYZ	1/15/2011	22.00	20.00				
XYZ	1/16/2011	21.00	19.00				
XYZ	1/17/2011	**20.50**	18.00				**18.00**
XYZ	1/18/2011	19.00	17.00				**17.00**
XYZ	1/19/2011	17.50	16.00				**16.00**
XYZ	1/20/2011	16.50	15.00	Trend Change Rule (a)		15.00	
XYZ	1/21/2011	15.50	14.00			14.00	
XYZ	1/22/2011	14.50	13.00			13.00	
XYZ	1/23/2011	13.50	12.00			12.00	
XYZ	1/24/2011	12.50	11.00			11.00	
XYZ	1/25/2011						
XYZ	1/26/2011						

Fig 8 Rally / Reac Trend Change (f)

XYZ

Sym	Date	High	Low	Nat Rally	Uptrend	Dntrend	Nat Reac
XYZ	1/1/2011	**22.00**	18.00				18.00
XYZ	1/2/2011	26.00	**23.00**	26.00	Rally		
XYZ	1/3/2011	27.00	**24.00**	27.00			
XYZ	1/4/2011	26.00	23.00				
XYZ	1/5/2011	25.00	22.00			Reaction	
XYZ	1/6/2011	24.00	21.00				
XYZ	1/7/2011	**23.00**	20.00				**20.00**
XYZ	1/8/2011	22.00	19.00				**19.00**
XYZ	1/9/2011	21.00	18.00				**18.00**
XYZ	1/10/2011	**20.00**	17.00				17.00
XYZ	1/11/2011	21.00	18.00				
XYZ	1/12/2011	22.00	19.00				
XYZ	1/13/2011	23.00	20.00	Rally			
XYZ	1/14/2011	24.00	**21.00**	**24.00**			
XYZ	1/15/2011	27.00	25.00	**27.00**			
XYZ	1/16/2011	29.00	27.00	**29.00**			
XYZ	1/17/2011	31.00	29.00		31.00	Trend Change Rule (b)	
XYZ	1/18/2011	33.00	31.00		33.00		
XYZ	1/19/2011						
XYZ	1/20/2011						
XYZ	1/21/2011						
XYZ	1/22/2011						
XYZ	1/23/2011						
XYZ	1/24/2011						
XYZ	1/25/2011						
XYZ	1/26/2011